GREGORY CORSO

M·I·N·D·F·I·E·L·D

New & Selected Poems

With forewords by

WILLIAM S. BURROUGHS
& ALLEN GINSBERG,

an introduction by

DAVID AMRAM,

and drawings by the author

Thunder's Mouth Press
New York

Published in the United States by
Thunder's Mouth Press
841 Broadway, Fourth Floor, New York, NY 10003

Library of Congress Cataloging-in-Publication Data
Corso, Gregory.
    Mindfield : new and selected poems.
    I. Title.
PS3505.0763A6   1989   811'.54   89-5152
ISBN 1-56025-201-4
Limited edition (alpha): 0-938410-90-3
Limited edition (numeric): 0-938410-96-2

The publisher wishes to thank Roger and Irvyne Richards, proprietors of the Rare Book Room, 125 Greenwich Avenue, New York, NY 10014 for their invaluable assistance in the compilation of this volume.

Grateful acknowledgement is also made to the New York State Council on the Arts and the National Endowment for the Arts for their assistance in the publication of this work.

Designed by Marcia Salo.

Printed in the United States of America.

Dedication

my son, Nile
   —I shall know you
      you me

for W.S. Burroughs
   —I know ye
      lovely bright ye

for Roger, Irvyne, and Hillary
   —slayers of homelessness,
      preservers of all lovely
      things—

Table of Contents

On Corso's Virtues

Gregory Corso's an aphoristic poet, and a poet of ideas. What modern poets write with such terse clarity that their verses stick in the mind without effort? Certainly Yeats, Pound, Williams, Eliot, Kerouac, Creeley, Dylan & Corso have that quality.

Corso's handling of ideas is unique, as in various one-word-title-poems ("Power", "Bomb", "Marriage", "Army", "Police", "Hair", "Death", "Clown" and later "Friend"). He distills the essence of archetypal concepts, recycling them with humor to make them new, examining, contrasting and alchemizing common vernacular notions into mindblowing (deconstructive or de-conditioning) insights. In this mode, his late 1950's poems (like Kerouac's 1951–52 scriptures on "Joan [Crawford] Rawshanks in the Fog" & "Neal and The Three Stooges") manifest a precursor Pop artistry, the realized notice of quotidian artifacts.

Poetic philosophe, Corso's uncanny insight mixes wisdom & logopoeia. "I'd a humor save me from amateur philosophy," he writes: "Fish is animalized water"—"knowing my words to be the acquainted prophecy of all men/and my unwords no less an acquaintanceship"— "Nothing sits on nothing in a nothing of many nothings a nothing king"—"I found God a gigantic fly paper"—"Standing on a street corner waiting for no one is Power"—"A star/is as far/as the eye/can see/and/as near/as my eye/is to me"—"And how can I trust them/who pollute the sky/with heavens/the below with hells."

As poetic craftsman, Corso is impeccable. His revision process, which he calls "tailoring," generally elision and condensation, yields gist-phrasing, extraordinary mind-jump humor. Clown sounds of circus, abstracted from plethora are reduced to perfect expression, "Tang-a-lang boom. Fife feef! Toot!" Quick sketch, sharp mind scissors.

As engineer of ideas, certain concepts recur retailored for nuance, such as "I shall never know my death," (i.e. dead he won't know it) and "You can't step in the same river once."

His late work, "The Whole Mess . . . Almost" is a masterpiece of Experience, the grand poetic abstractions Truth, Love, God, Faith Hope Charity, Beauty, money, Death, & Humor are animated in a single poem with brilliant & intimate familiarity.

As poetic wordslinger he has command of idiomatic simplicity, to wit: "A hat is power," "fried shoes" or:

> O Bomb I love you
> I want to kiss your clank   eat your boom
> You are a paean an acme of scream
> a lyric hat of Mister Thunder

as well as exuberant invention as "an astrologer dabbling in dragon prose":

> . . . Bomb
> from your belly outflock vulturic salutations
> Battle forth your spangled hyena finger stumps
> along the brink of Paradise

Corso also excels as political philosophe; his many years as classic artist wanderer dwelling in European hotels, castles, & streets gives him perspective on North America. His crucial position in world cultural revolution mid-XX century as originator of the "Beat Generation" literary movement, along with Kerouac, Burroughs, Orlovsky and others, grants him an experience inside history few bards or politicians have known. Readers of the poem cluster "Elegiac Feelings American" will appreciate Corso's generational insight into Empire sickness. Earlier poems like "Power," "Bomb", "Army", & many brief expatriate lyrics prove Corso to be Shelley's natural prophet among "unacknowledged legislators of the world."

Corso is a poet's Poet, his verse pure velvet, close to John Keats for our time, exquisitely delicate in manners of the Muse. He has been and always will be a popular poet, awakener of youth, puzzlement & pleasure for sophisticated elder bibliophiles, "Immortal" as immortal is, Captain Poetry exampling revolution of Spirit, his "poetry the opposite of hypocrisy," a loner, laughably unlaurelled by native prizes, divine Poet Maudit, rascal poet Villonesque and Rimbaudian whose wild fame's extended for decades around the world from France to China, World poet.

March 1989   Allen Ginsberg

Introductory Notes

Someone asked Samuel Beckett what he thought of William Burroughs, and he reportedly replied, somewhat grudgingly: "Well, he's a writer." I have always cherished the compliment.

And I can say, ungrudgingly: Gregory Corso is a poet. He has the rare calling of a pure lyric gift. And he has never doubted his calling.

I first met Gregory in Allen Ginsberg's apartment on East 7th Street in New York, in 1953. At this time I had just returned from an expedition in search of *yagé* in South America. My only published work was *Junky.* Allen told me about this gifted young poet who was to arrive momentarily and fix breakfast for us. Gregory arrived and burned the toast. When I upbraided him with unnecessary asperity, he said, in effect, that after all, he was a *poet.*

After that I saw Gregory from time to time at Allen's, and in the San Remo Bar. There was a special quality about him, a radiant, childlike charm. I did not at that time appreciate the quality of his poetry. Recognition came much later, in Paris, when Brion Gysin, Sinclair Beiles, Gregory, and your reporter were working on *Minutes to Go.* Brion was knocked out by Gregory's poems, and quite suddenly I saw and heard and realized: Gregory *is* a poet.

Little incidents come to mind. We ordered wild boar in a French restaurant around the corner from rue Git-le-Coeur, where we all stayed. When the wild boar arrived, Gregory took one sniff and refused to taste it. I chided him overbearingly for being provincial, and took a mouthful myself—and came near to spitting it right out on the plate, with the words of Samuel Johnson when he spat out some over-hot food: "A fool would have swallowed that." It had a horrible, rank musky taste. But I did gag down one mouthful for the experience.

As I said, Gregory has never doubted his calling. Years ago, when he called W. H. Auden on the phone, Auden said:

"Who is *this?*"

"Gregory."

"Gregory *who?*"

"Gregory *the poet!*"

Auden, in his prime, donnish valiance, would have none of it. I think he felt that it was vaguely indecent—"Girls from one to ten/Beware of Englishmen."—or at least in questionable taste, to call oneself a *poet.*

"What have I done?/A lamb mess drawing flies."

The English knee-jerk liberal, who threw a shoe when Gregory read "Bomb," will never understand poetry or poets, for poetic reality has nothing to do with political or social reality.

And Gregory has another rare gift: he has a voice. When you think of Gregory, you will hear his voice. This is not always an endearing gift but it becomes Gregory, because the voice is good. Gregory's voice echoes through a precarious future. It will be heard so long as there is anyone there to listen.

There are those who say that Gregory has grave flaws of character. Poetry is made from flaws. A flawless poet is fit only to be a poet-laureate, officially dead and inperfectly embalmed. The stink of death leaks out: "Rarely, if once, will Nature give/The power to be a Laureate and live."—(with apologies to E. A. Robinson)

I think that Gregory would survive even the laurel crown, for the smell of *life* would leak out.

I stroll through Gregory's poems, stopping here and there: ah, yes, I remember you, and you, and you . . . We all stop in different places, but there are stopping places for anyone who knows what poetry is:

> Fierce, with mustaches of gold
> Guns rusting in arthritic hands

Don't shoot the warthog!
Pasting posters of mercy
On the stark posts of despair
A young child doomed by his sombrero
The cactus outlives you
Dirty Eyes aims a knife at me
I pump him full of soft watches
A favorite doll
Buried in the attic, it dies forever
Here, touch my electric hand
Laughter dies long after jest
The joker smiles no joke
He had no foes, he made them all into *friends*
Some friends want to be everybody's friends
Some friends always want to do you favors
Some always want to get *near* you
Those who haven't any friends and want them are creepy
Those who have friends and don't want them are doomed
Those who haven't any friends and don't want them are
    grand
Does one need a friend in heaven?
The mean cat in a little dark corner
Trembles the entire room
And so I gave the Gods away
And thought is all I know of Death . . .

Gregory is a gambler. He suffers reverses, like every man who takes chances. But his vitality and resilience always shine through, with a light that is more than human: the immortal light of his Muse.

Gregory is indeed one of the Daddies.

March 1989   William S. Burroughs

Introduction

When I met Gregory Corso in 1956, Jack Kerouac and I were already performing together at bring-your-own-bottle loft parties in lower Manhattan. I had never heard him read and had not read any of his poetry.

Allen Ginsberg, whom I met in 1955 when I was playing with Charles Mingus, had talked to me about Gregory. "He is the poet you have to read, David," Allen said to me. "I like his work even more than my own." I hadn't read Allen's poetry either, but I admired his devotion to Gregory's work, just as many of us still appreciate Allen's efforts to help get Jack Kerouac's timeless poetic prose novels published.

Like Jack, Corso was comfortable in the milieu of the mid 1950s community of jazz musicians. He was respectful of the music and musicians who created spontaneous and sophisticated improvisations that soared beyond the restrictions of a conformist society that considered all of us to be schizophrenic nut cases and terminal losers. What all of us had in common with Gregory was boundless energy, outrageous individualism, and the ability to laugh a lot when confronted by overly cerebral intellectuals who wanted creative people in America to act like morticians.

When I first heard Gregory read and then began reading his poems, some of which he gave me (his 1957 "Thanksgiving" which he signed to me and which I'll always treasure), I saw a kindred spirit. Like Kerouac, Gregory saw the beauty and poetic facets of everyday life that most of America ignored. Tiny fragments of everyday conversations, whispered secrets, broken promises, and soaring flights of his imagination inspired Gregory to create a body of work that shines alone, as clear and pure as the classic jazz solos that enriched the world forever and provided a milieu for all of us in the arts during the 1950s.

Fortunately, Gregory wrote his poems down. Like the improvised solos that were recorded by the jazz masters, Gregory's poems stand the test of time. They are still as fresh to the reader or listener today as they were when they were first created. As a performer Gregory was often so outrageous that the audience forgot to pay attention to his poems. Like Kerouac, he never sought the limelight. He wanted people to read his work. He was also a spellbinding reader of his poetry when he was alone in a room with you.

In 1959 we appeared together in the film "Pull My Daisy." Gregory's antics and spontaneous raps kept the entire cast screaming with laughter for the weeks we were together.

It was a silent film, narrated after its completion by Kerouac, accompanied by my music. Forty years later, Gregory's performance still has a resonance, as the crazed poet visionary. He did not have to act. He was simply being his irrepressible self.

As the years passed, Gregory continued to create gems taken from his life experiences. In 1965, I bumped into Gregory, Neal Cassidy, Allen, and Peter Orlovsky in San Francisco, where a cantata I had written with poet Langston Hughes was receiving its world premier at the San Francisco Opera House.

"I love the piece," said Gregory after the concert. "Langston's poetry came through the way you set it for the chorus, soloists, and the symphony. It's beautiful work, man, but get rid of that white tie and tails you're wearing. You look like an out-of-work doorman or Count Dracula about to jump out of his coffin."

In the 70s and 80s, Gregory persevered, and in the 90s the interest by young people in Kerouac's work opened the door for Gregory and his life's work to be rediscovered by a whole new generation. Like Ferlinghetti, Robert Creeley, Diane DiPrima, Gary Snyder, Bob Kaufman, and a host of other poets of our era, he never gave up, sold out, or forgot what he wanted to express and who he was.

We still stay in touch, and share messages of admiration and respect from young musicians, poets, painters, actors, dancers, and all kinds of people who love his work and are moved by his spirit. When they ask me, after my concerts, to call him, I always do. It is a joy to share the appreciation of others with him.

In a world of computers, cyberspace, high tech shlock, and instant trash, Gregory Corso's poems shine. He has a voice of his own, and it rings clear and true.

As his fellow poet Shelley said long ago, "A thing of beauty is a joy forever." It is cause to rejoice with the publication of this collection of poetry.

David Amram
August 1998

From **THE VESTAL LADY ON BRATTLE**

Greenwich Village Suicide

Arms outstretched
hands flat against the windowsides
She looks down
Thinks of Bartok, Van Gogh
And New Yorker cartoons
She falls

They take her away with a Daily News on her face
And a storekeeper throws hot water on the sidewalk

In the Morgue

a dream

I remember seeing their pictures in the papers;
Naked, they seemed stronger.
The bullet in my stomach proved that I was dead.
I watched the embalmer unscrew the glass top.
He examined me and smiled at my minute-dead-life
Then he went back to the two bodies across from me
And continued to unscrew.

When you're dead you can't talk
Yet you feel like you could.
It was funny watching those two gangsters across from me
        trying to talk.
They widened their thin lips and showed grey-blue teeth;

The embalmer, still smiling, came back to me.
He picked me up and like a mother would a child,
Rested me upright in a rocking chair.
He gave a push and I rocked.
Being dead didn't mean much.
I still felt pain where the bullet went through.

God! seeing the two gangsters from this angle was really
        strange!
They certainly didn't look like they looked in the papers.
Here they were young and clean shaven and well-shaped.

Sea Chanty

My mother hates the sea

my sea especially

I warned her not to

it was all I could do

Two years later

the sea ate her

Upon the shore I found a strange

yet beautiful food

I asked the sea if I could eat it

and the sea said that I could

—Oh, sea, what fish is this

so tender and so sweet?

—Thy mother's feet

Song

Oh, dear! Oh, me! Oh, my!
I married the pig's daughter!
I married the pig's daughter!

Why? Why? Why?

I met her in the evening
in the moon in the sky!
She kissed me in the evening
and wed me in her sty!
Oh, dear! Oh, me! Oh, my!
I married the pig's daughter!
I married the pig's daughter!

Why? Why? Why?

Because I felt I had oughta!
Because I was the one that taught her
how to love and how to die!
And tomorrow there'll be no sorrow
no, there'll be no sorrow
when I take her to the slaughter!
When I take her to the slaughter!

Why? Why? Why?

The Horse Was Milked

In a room a spoon upon the fire
was cooking his secret desire

When all was cooked he got a belt
and hurried before the horse could melt.

He strapped the belt across his arm;
wiped the needle so it'd not harm

and tightened, tightened the belt for a vein.
He pulled and his arm began to pain.

With steadied hand he waited the bulge—
waited the dream in which he'd indulge.

And it came, and the needle filled it with joy.
But the horse was milked, and there was no joy.

He fell to the floor without a sound,
and rolled his head like a merry-go-round.

Then he rubbed and shook and yanked his hair,
and vomited air, nothing but air.

Deep in the night he rolled and groaned.
O never was a poor soul so stoned.

Requiem for
"Bird" Parker, Musician

this prophecy came by mail:
in the last murder of birds
a nowhere bird shall remain
and it shall not wail
and the nowhere bird shall be a slow bird
a long long bird

somewhere there is a room
in a room
in which an old horn
   lies in a corner
like a handful of rice
wondering about BIRD

   first voice

hey, man, BIRD is dead
they got his horn locked up somewhere
put his horn in a corner somewhere
like where's the horn, man, where?

   second voice

screw the horn
like where's BIRD?

   third voice

gone
BIRD was goner than sound
broke the barrier with a horn's coo
BIRD was higher than moon

BIRD hovered on a roof top, too
like a weirdy monk he dropped
horn in hand, high above all
lookin' down on them people
with half-shut weirdy eyes
saying to himself: "yeah, yeah"
like nothin' meant nothin' at all

fourth voice

in early nightdrunk
solo in his pent house stand
BIRD held a black flower in his black hand
he blew his horn to the sky
made the sky fantastic! and midway
the man-tired use of things
BIRD piped a varied ephemera
a strained rhythmical rat
like the stars didn't know what to do
then came a nowhere bird

third voice

yeah, a nowhere bird—
while BIRD was blowin'
another bird came
an unreal bird
a nowhere bird with big draggy wings
BIRD paid it no mind; just kept on blowin'
and the cornball bird came on comin'

first voice

right, like that's what I heard
the draggy bird landed in front of BIRD
looked BIRD straight in the eye
BIRD said: "cool it"
and kept on blowin'

second voice

seems like BIRD put the square bird down

first voice

only for a while, man
the nowhere bird began to foam from the mouth
making all kinds of discords
"man, like make it elsewhere," BIRD implored
but the nowhere bird paced back and forth
like an old cornball with a nowhere scheme

third voice

yeah, by that time BIRD realized the fake
had come to goof
BIRD was about to split, when all of a sudden
the nowhere bird sunk its beady head
into the barrel of BIRD's horn
bugged, BIRD blew a long crazy note

first voice

it was his last, man, his last
the draggy bird ran death into BIRD's throat
and the whole building rumbled
when BIRD let go his horn
and the sky got blacker . . . blacker
and the nowhere bird wrapped its muddy wings round BIRD
brought BIRD down
all the way down

fourth voice

BIRD is dead
BIRD is dead

first and second and third voices

yeah, yeah

      fourth voice

wail for BIRD
for BIRD is dead

      first and second and third voices

yeah, yeah

12 Ash St. Place

That house is a ghost of pretty things

like to the solitaire of a bird

a natural pity broods there

There's an old man who always sits by candlelight

I can see his hands move

dripping colors crushed ones

like pressed flowers dropped from a book

I passed his window one day

got a closer look at him

. . . he must have been a hundred years old

I asked him if he thought it would rain

he said:—No—and dripped a purple color on my hand

Walking away

I told him I didn't think that was nice of him

. . . because the color burned

The Wreck of the Nordling

One night fifty men swam away from God

And drowned

In the morning the abandoned God

Dipped His finger into the sea

Came up with fifty souls

And pointed towards eternity

A Pastoral Fetish

Old Mac Donald wears clod-hoppers
in his walk through field of lilac and dandelion
A storm-trooper, like a Klee twittering machine, he stomps:
Crunch one lilac here; crunch another dandelion there,
here, there, everywhere (he's got no mercy at all)
crunch crunch here and a crunch crunch there
crunch everywhere . . .

There comes a time when he's got to stop
take off his shoes; go to bed . . .
ah, that's when Old MacDonald's in his glory.
Green blood and mud-caked leather he digs the most.
He makes it a habit to sleep his nose by his toes
so that all night long he could snore in the sticky smell
of murdered lilac and dandelion.
It's the old bastard's greatest kick.

St. Luke's, Service for Thomas

The White Horse innkeeper
Leaned nervously against the stained-glass;
He shifted his feet, and Cummings mourned by.

A sightseer whispered into a sightseeing ear.
And a Swansea woman entered . . .

Two neon-villagers underarmed her;
Sat her down in the first row.
She raised her head, and peered
. . . The body wasn't there.

The service ended in illimitable whispers.

A Ceylonese prince was first to leave.
He waited by the church gate
And little groups gathered, chattered.

Across the street the school children
Were playing tag-ball.
The ball rolled in front of the innkeeper;
He kicked it hard
And strode back to his inn.

Cambridge, First Impressions

1

It is not easy to walk
    these Cambridge streets
Better carpets make it difficult.

Yet in masquerade I slip unnoticed within the parade
And my walk is slightly eased.
How great it is to be heralded in walking!

But my lie makes awkward the gait.
Out of step, my identity is revealed.
The ash-foot sentinels
    on every Cambridge corner
    stand too severe;
Their clarion-warnings discord
    the rhythms I walk to hear.

2

Yet Cambridge is not all banner and majesty,
On the side lines
    I watch the rhythmic embassy—
    Brattle and all its accoutrements—
Give up their rigid themes
Forsake their regnant march
Roll up the carpets,
    go home.

Home, and the streets are unnatural.
Walking, I catch Cambridge in a seldom jubilee:—
     Vivaldi, Getz, Bach and Dizzy,
     in a melody all together contained,
     emerge, like twining wisps of smoke,
     from out parlors and cellars,
Jumping the chestnuts in Longfellow;
Sprinting down Hawthorne,
Swinging through Lowell,
And flying real-crazy over Dana.

3

Morning, and it is terrible to walk.
Once again the sentinels are stationed;
     their clarions pied-pipe
     the streets clean of the jubilant night-rats,
And quickly the better carpets spread.

4

The old bastard lied that told me Melville
     visioned lots of times while walking
     in the early morning,
     separate from the carpets and parade, on Brattle.
I've walked Brattle lots of these days,
     and not once did I catch from out the dark
     a line of light.

He said:—Walk, man, walk that crazy Revolutionary road,
     old Brattle;
You'll dig the greatest visions ever;
Man, like Melville visioned Moby Dick right on Brattle!
Right in the middle of the street!

5

Tired of walking,
Tired of seeing nothing,
I look out from a window
     belonging to someone
     nice enough to let me look.

And from a window Cambridge is not all that bad.
It is a great feeling to know
     that from a window
I can go to books to cans of beer to past loves.
And from these gather enough dream
     to sneak out a back door.

From **GASOLINE**

In the Fleeting Hand of Time

On the steps of the bright madhouse
I hear the bearded bell shaking down the woodlawn
the final knell of my world
I climb and enter a firey gathering of knights
they unaware of my presence lay forth sheepskin plans
and with mailcoated fingers trace my arrival
back back back when on the black steps of Nero lyre Rome
    I stood
in my arms the wailing philosopher
the final call of mad history
Now my presence is known
my arrival marked by illuminated stains
The great windows of Paradise open
Down to radiant dust fall the curtains of Past Time
In fly flocks of multicolored birds
Light winged light O the wonder of light
Time takes me by the hand
born March 26, 1930 I am led 100 mph o'er the vast market
    of choice
what to choose? what to choose?
O — — — and I leave my orange room of myth
no chance to lock away my toys of Zeus
I choose the room of Bleecker Street
A baby mother stuffs my mouth with a pale Milanese breast
I suck I struggle I cry O Olympian mother
unfamiliar this breast to me
Snows
Decade of icy asphalt doomed horses
Weak dreams   Dark corridors of P.S.42   Roofs   Ratthroated
    pigeons
Led 100 mph over these all too real Mafia streets
profanely I shed my Hermean wings

O Time be merciful
throw me beneath your humanity of cars
feed me to giant grey skyscrapers
exhaust my heart to your bridges
I discard my lyre of Orphic futility

And for such betrayal I climb these bright mad steps
and enter this room of paradisical light
ephemeral
Time
a long long dog having chased its orbited tail
comes grab my hand
and leads me into conditional life

Amnesia in Memphis

Who am I, flat beneath the shades of Isis,
This clay-skinned body, made study
by the physicians of Memphis?
Was it always my leaving the North
Snug on the back of the crocodile?
Do I remember this whorl of mummy cloth
As I stood fuming by the Nile?
O life abandoned! half-embalmed, I beat the soil!
For what I am; who I am, I cannot regain,
Nor sponge my life back with the charm of Ibis oil—
Still-omen of the dribbling Scarab!
Fate that leads me into the chamber of blue perfumes!
Is there no other worthy of prophecy
Than that Decker who decks my spine with ostrich plumes?

No more will the scurvy Sphinx
With beggy prophets their prophecies relate—

Mexican Impressions

I

Through a moving window
I see a glimpse of burros
    a Pepsi Cola stand,
an old Indian sitting
    smiling toothless by a hut.

II

Stopping at Guaymas,
a brand new Ford pick-up
filled with melancholy laborers;
in the driver's seat, a young child
—doomed by his sombrero.

III

Windmill, silverwooded, slatless, motionless in Mexico—
Birdlike incongruous windmill, like a broken crane,
One-legged, stiff, arbitrary, with wide watchful eye,
How did you happen here?—All alone, alien, helpless,
Here where there is no wind?
Living gaunt structure resigned, are you pleased
    with this dry windless monkage?
Softer, the cactus outlives you.

IV

I tell you, Mexico—
I think miles and miles of dead full-bodièd horses—
Thoroughbreds and work horses, flat on their sides
Stiffened with straight legs and lipless mouths.
It is the stiff leg, Mexico, the jutted tooth,
That wrecks my equestrian dreams of nightmare.

V

In the Mexican Zoo
    they have ordinary
American cows.

Sun

automatic poem

Sun hypnotic! holy ball protracted long and sure! firey
    goblet! day-babble!
Sun, sun-webbed heat! tropic goblet dry! spider thirst! Sun,
    unwater!
Sun misery sun ire sun sick sun dead sun rot sun relic!
Sun o'er Afric sky low and tipped, spilt, almost empty,
    hollow vial, sunbone, sunstone, iron sun, sundial.
Sun dinosaur of electric motion extinct and fossiled, babble
    on!
Sun, season of the season, catching actual sunfish, on the
    green shore sunbathing like a madness.
Sun eros hellish superreal conglomeration of miasmatic ire!
Sun, sun-downed beings in desert life astounded, go down!
Sun circus! tent of helion, apollo, rha, sol, sun, exhult!
The sun like a blazing ship went down in Teliphicci lake.
The sun like a blazing disc of jelly slid over the Teliphiccian
    alps.
The sun leads the night and follows the night and leads the
    night.
The sun can be chariot-driven.
The sun like a blazing lollipop can be sucked.
The sun is shaped like a curved beckoning finger.
The sun spins walks dances skips runs.
The sun favors palm citrics tubercular-lungs
The sun eats up Teliphicci lake and alps every rising.
The sun does not know what it is to like or dislike.
The sun all my life went down in Teliphicci lake.
O constant hole where all beyond is true Byzantium.

Puma in Chapultepec Zoo

Long smooth slow swift soft cat
What score, whose choreography did you dance to
    when they pulled the final curtain down?
Can such ponderous grace remain
    here, all alone, on this 9×10 stage?
Will they give you another chance
    perhaps to dance the Sierras?
How sad you seem; looking at you
    I think of Ulanova
    locked in some small furnished room
    in New York, on East 17th Street
    in the Puerto Rican section.

Botticelli's "Spring"

No sign of Spring!
Florentine sentinels
   from icy campanili
watch for a sign—
    Lorenzo dreams to awaken bluebirds
    Ariosto sucks his thumb.
    Michelangelo sits forward on his bed
    . . . awakened by no new change.
    Dante pulls back his velvet hood,
    his eyes are deep and sad.
    His great dane weeps.
No sign of Spring!
    Leonardo paces his unbearable room
    . . . holds an arrogant eye on die-hard snow.
    Raffaelo steps into a warm bath
     . . . his long silken hair is dry
    because of lack of sun.
    Aretino remembers Spring in Milan; his mother,
    who now, on sweet Milanese hills, sleeps.
No sign of Spring! No sign!
Ah, Botticelli opens the door of his studio.

Uccello

They will never die on that battlefield
nor the shade of wolves recruit their hoard like brides of
wheat on all horizons   waiting there to consume battle's end
There will be no dead to tighten their loose bellies
no heap of starched horses to redsmash their bright eyes
or advance their eat of dead
They would rather hungersulk with mad tongues
than believe that on that field no man dies.

They will never die who fight so embraced
breath to breath   eye knowing eye   impossible to die
or move   no light seeping through   no maced arm
nothing but horse outpanting horse   shield brilliant upon
shield   all made starry by the dot ray of a helmeted eye
ah   how difficult to fall between those knitted lances
And those banners! angry as to flush insignia across its
erasure of sky
You'd think he'd paint his armies by the coldest rivers
have rows of iron skulls flashing in the dark
You'd think it impossible for any man to die
each combatant's mouth is a castle of song
each iron fist a dreamy gong   flail resounding flail
like cries of gold
how I dream to join such battle!
a silver man on a black horse with red standard and striped
lance   never to die but to be endless
a golden prince of pictorial war

On the Walls
of a Dull Furnished Room

I hang old photos of my childhood girls—
with breaking heart I sit, elbow on table,
Chin on hand, studying
      the proud eyes of Helen,
      the golden hair of Susan,
      the weak mouth of Jane.

Italian Extravaganza

Mrs. Lombardi's month-old son is dead.
I saw it in Rizzo's funeral parlor,
A small purplish wrinkled head.

They've just finished having high mass for it;
They're coming out now
. . . wow, such a small coffin!
And ten black cadillacs to haul it in.

Birthplace Revisited

I stand in the dark light in the dark street
and look up at my window, I was born there.
The lights are on; other people are moving about.
I am with raincoat; cigarette in mouth,
hat over eye,
I cross the street and enter the building.
The garbage cans haven't stopped smelling.
I walk up the first flight; Dirty Ears
aims a knife at me . . .
I pump him full of lost watches.

The Last Gangster

Waiting by the window
my feet enwrapped with the dead bootleggers of Chicago
I am the last gangster, safe, at last,
waiting by a bullet-proof window.

I look down the street and know
the two torpedoes from St. Louis.
I've watched them grow old
. . . guns rusting in their arthritic hands.

But I Do Not Need Kindness

I have known the strange nurses of Kindness,
I have seen them kiss the sick, attend the old,
give candy to the mad!
I have watched them, all night, dark and sad,
rolling wheelchairs by the sea!
I have known the fat pontiffs of Kindness,
the little old grey-haired lady,
the neighborhood priest,
the famous poet,
the mother,
I have known them all!
I have watched them, at night, dark and sad,
pasting posters of mercy
        on the stark posts of despair.

2

I have known Almighty Kindness Herself!
I have sat beside Her pure white feet,
gaining Her confidence!
We spoke of nothing unkind,
but one night I was tormented by those strange nurses,
those fat pontiffs
The little old lady rode a spiked car over my head!
The priest cut open my stomach, put his hands in me,
and cried:—Where's your soul? Where's your soul!—
The famous poet picked me up
and threw me out of the window!
The mother abandoned me!
I ran to Kindness, broke into Her chamber,
and profaned!
with an unnamable knife I gave Her a thousand wounds,
and inflicted them with filth!

I carried Her away, on my back, like a ghoul!
down the cobble-stoned night!
Dogs howled! Cats fled! All windows closed!
I carried Her ten flights of stairs!
Dropped Her on the floor of my small room,
and kneeling beside Her, I wept. I wept.

3

But what is Kindness? I have killed Kindness,
but what is it?
You are kind because you live a kind life.
St. Francis was kind.
The landlord is kind.
A cane is kind.
Can I say people, sitting in parks, are kinder?

Don't Shoot the Warthog

A child came to me
swinging an ocean on a stick.
He told me his sister was dead,
I pulled down his pants
and gave him a kick.
I drove him down the streets
down the night of my generation
I screamed his name, his cursed name,
down the streets of my generation
and children lept in joy to the name
and running came.
Mothers and fathers bent their heads to hear;
I screamed the name.

The child trembled, fell,
and staggered up again,
I screamed his name!
And a fury of mothers and fathers
sank their teeth into his brain.
I called to the angels of my generation
on the rooftops, in the alleyways,
beneath the garbage and the stones,
I screamed the name! and they came
and gnawed the child's bones.
I screamed the name: Beauty
Beauty   Beauty   Beauty

I Am 25

With a love a madness for Shelley
Chatterton   Rimbaud
and the needy-yap of my youth
       has gone from ear to ear:
    I HATE OLD POETMEN!
Especially old poetmen who retract
who consult other old poetmen
who speak their youth in whispers,
saying:—I did those then
       but that was then
       that was then—
O I would quiet old men
say to them:—I am your friend
       what you once were, thru me
       you'll be again—
Then at night in the confidence of their homes
rip out their apology-tongues
       and steal their poems.

Three

1

The streetsinger is sick
crouched in the doorway, holding his heart.

One less song in the noisy night.

2

Outside the wall
the aged gardener plants his shears
A new young man
has come to snip the hedge

3

Death weeps because Death is human
spending all day in a movie when a child dies.

Hello

It is disastrous to be a wounded deer.
I'm the most wounded, wolves stalk,
and I have my failures, too.
My flesh is caught on the Inevitable Hook!
As a child I saw many things I did not want to be.
Am I the person I did not want to be?
That talks-to-himself person?
That neighbors-make-fun-of person?
Am I he who, on museum steps, sleeps on his side?
Do I wear the cloth of a man who has failed?
Am I the looney man?
In the great serenade of things,
    am I the most cancelled passage?

The Mad Yak

I am watching them churn the last milk
    they'll ever get from me.
They are waiting for me to die;
They want to make buttons out of my bones.
Where are my sisters and brothers?
That tall monk there, loading my uncle,
    he has a new cap.
And that idiot student of his—
    I never saw that muffler before.
Poor uncle, he lets them load him.
How sad he is, how tired!
I wonder what they'll do with his bones?
And that beautiful tail!
How many shoelaces will they make of that!

This Was My Meal

In the peas I saw upside down letters of MONK
And beside it, in the Eyestares of Wine
I saw Olive & Blackhair
   I decided sunset to dine

I cut through the cowbrain and saw Christmas
& my birthday run hand in hand in the snow
I cut deeper
   and Christmas bled to the edge of the plate

I turned to my father
   and he ate my birthday
I drank my milk and saw trees outrun themselves
   valleys outdo themselves
     and no mountain stood a chance of not walking

Dessert came in the spindly hands of stepmother
I wanted to drop fire-engines from my mouth!
But in ran the moonlight and grabbed the prunes.

For Miles

Your sound is faultless
    pure & round
        holy
    almost profound

Your sound is your sound
    true & from within
    a confession
    soulful & lovely

Poet whose sound is played
    lost or recorded
    but heard
    can you recall that 54 night at the Open Door
    when you & bird
    wailed five in the morning some wondrous
    yet unimaginable score?

Doll Poem

A favorite doll
knows the pain of a child's farewell.
Buried in the crib in the attic it dies forever.
Candy-colors fade
long pants lead us elsewhere
and a child's hands are getting hair.
Chewed-pencils, clips, pennies in our pockets
where are they?
The child's body is longer
long as the earth
everybody walks on him, some on wheelchairs,
long mad envious journey.
Soda and fig-newtons will erupt from the mouth.

Last Night I Drove a Car

a dream

Last night I drove a car
      not knowing how to drive
      not owning a car
I drove and knocked down
      people I loved
      . . . went 120 through one town.

I stopped at Hedgeville
      and slept in the back seat
      . . . excited about my new life.

Zizi's Lament

I am in love with the laughing sickness
it would do me a lot of good if I had it—
I have worn the splendid gowns of Sudan,
carried the magnificent halivas of Boudodin Bros.,
kissed the singing Fatimas of the pimp of Aden,
wrote glorious psalms in Hakhaliba's cafe,
but I've never had the laughing sickness,
so what good am I?

The fat merchant offers me opium, kief, hashish,
        even camel juice,
all is unsatisfactory—
O bitter damned night! you again! must I yet
pluck out my unreal teeth
undress my unlaughable self
put to sleep this melancholy head?
I am nothing without the laughing sickness.

My father's got it, my grandfather had it;
surely my Uncle Fez will get it, but me, me
who it would do the most good,
will I ever get it?

From **THE HAPPY BIRTHDAY OF DEATH**

Notes After Blacking Out

Lady of the legless world I have
　　refused to go beyond self-disappearance
I'm in the thin man's bed knowing my legs
　　kept to me by a cold fresh air
Useless and not useless this meaning
All is answerable I need not know the answer
Poetry is seeking the answer
Joy is in knowing there is an answer
Death is knowing the answer
(That faint glow in the belly of Enlightment
　　is the dead spouting their answers)

Queen of cripples the young no longer
　　seem necessary
The old are secretive about their Know
They are constant additions to this big
　　unauthorized lie
Yet Truth's author itself is nothingness
And though I make it vital that nothingness
　　itself will collapse
There is nothing.
Nothing ever was
Nothing is a house never bought
Nothing comes after this wildbright Joke
Nothing sits on nothing in a nothing of many nothings
　　a nothing king

How Happy I Used to Be

How happy I used to be
imagining myself so many things—
    Alexander Hamilton lying in the snow
    shoe buckles rusting in the snow
    pistol shot crushing his brow.
Behind a trail of visiting kings
I cried:
    Will Venice and Genoa
    give welcome as did Verona?
    I have no immediate chateau
    for the Duke of Genoa
    no African bull for the Doge of Venice
    but for the Pope!
    I have the hideout of the Turk.
    Informer? No—I'm in it
    for the excitement;
    between Afghanistan and Trinidad
    intrigue and opera are electrified
    everywhere is electricity!
The mad spinning ballerina
sees me in the audience and falls into a faint,
    I smile I smile I smile—
Or yesterday when I heard a sad song
I stopped to hear and wept
for when had I last imagined myself a king
a kind king with ambassadors and flowers and wise teachers—
What has happened to me now that
everything has been fulfilled?
Will I again walk up Lexington Avenue
or down it
feeling warm to Richard the Third
and the executioner
whose black hood is oppressive to wear?

Am I not music walking behind Ben Franklin
music in his two loaves of bread
and Massachusetts half-penny?
I knew 1768 when all was patched eyes and wooden legs
How happy I was fingering pieces of eight, doubloons—
Children, have you not heard of my meeting
with Israel Hans, Israel Hans—

Seaspin

To drown to be slow hair
To be fish minstrelry
One eye to flick and stare
The fathomed wreck to see—
Forever down to drown
Descend the squid's conclave
Black roof the whale's belly
Oyster floor the grave—

My sea-ghost rise
And slower hair
Silverstreaks my eyes
Up up I whirl
And wonder where—

To breathe in Neptune's cup
Nudge gale and tempest
Feel the mermaid up
To stay to pin my hair
On the sea-horse's stirrup—

Hair

My beautiful hair is dead
Now I am the rawhead
O when I look in the mirror
the bald I see is balder still
When I sleep the sleep I sleep
is not at will
And when I dream I dream children waving goodbye—
It was lovely hair once
it was
Hours before shop windows   gum-machine mirrors   with great
                                                         combs

pockets filled with jars of lanolin
Washed hair I hated
With dirt the waves came easier and stayed
Yet nothing would rid me of dandruff
Vitalis Lucky-Tiger Wildroot Brilliantine   nothing—
To lie in bed and be hairless is a blunder only God could allow—
The bumps on my head—I wouldn't mind being bald
if the bumps on my head made people sorry—
Careless God! Now how can old ladies cookie me?
How to stand thunderous on an English cliff
a hectic Heathcliff?
O my lovely stained-glass hair is dry   dark   invisible
not there!
Sun! it is you who are to blame!
And to think I once held my hair to you
like a rich proud silk merhant—
Bald! I'm bald!
Best now I get a pipe
and forget girls.

Subways take me one of your own
seat me anybody
let me off any station anyman
What use my walking up Fifth Ave
or going to theatre for intermission
or standing in front of girls schools
when there is nothing left for me to show—
Wrestlers are bald
And though I'm thin O God give me chance now to wrestle
or even be a Greek wrestler with a bad heart
and make that heart make me sweat
—my head swathed in towels in an old locker room
that I speak good English before I die—
Barbers are murdered in the night!
Razors and scissors are left in rain!
No hairdresser dare scheme a new shampoo!
No premature hair on the babe's pubis!
Wigmaker! help me! my fingernails are knived in your door!
I want a wig of winter's vast network!
A beard of hogs snouting acorns!
Samson bear with me! Just a moustache
and I'd surmount governance over Borneo!
O even a nose hair, an ingrown hair,
and I'd tread beauty a wicked foot, ah victory!
Useless useless
I must move away from sun
Live elsewhere
—a bald body dressed in old lady cloth.
O the fuzzy wuzzy grief!
Mercy, wreathed this coldly lonely head a crowning glory!
I stand in darkness
weeping to angels washing their oceans of hair.
There goes my hair! shackled to a clumping wind!

Come back, hair, come back!
I want to grow sideburns!
I want to wash you, comb you, sun you, love you!
as I ran from you wild before—
I thought surely this nineteen hundred and fifty nine of now
that I need no longer bite my fingernails
but have handsome gray hair
to show how profoundly nervous I am.

Damned be hair!
Hair that must be plucked from soup!
Hair that clogs the bathtub!
Hair that costs a dollar fifty to be murdered!
Disgusting hair! eater of peroxide! dye! sand!
Monks and their bagel heads!
Ancient Egypt and their mops!
Negroes and their stocking caps!
Armies! Universities! Industries! and their branded crews!
Antoinette Du Barry Pompadour and their platinum cakes!
Veronica Lake   Truman Capote   Ishka Bibble   Messiahs   Paganinis
Bohemians   Hawaiians   poodles

Under Peyote

The flower that bounces sneaking through a
door holding a girl from home
with
    a new light
  a bannister of music
The difference of minutes

      for

           summer
           children

             target

                 bacteria

Transformation & Escape

1

I reached heaven and it was syrupy.
It was oppressively sweet.
Croaking substances stuck to my knees.
Of all substances St. Michael was stickiest.
I grabbed him and pasted him on my head.
I found God a gigantic fly paper.
I stayed out of his way.
I walked where everything smelled of burnt chocolate.
Meanwhile St. Michael was busy with his sword
hacking away at my hair.
I found Dante standing naked in a blob of honey.
Bears were licking his thighs.
I snatched St. Michael's sword
and quartered myself in a great circular adhesive.
My torso fell upon an elastic equilibrium.
As though shot from a sling
my torso whizzed at God fly paper.
My legs sank into some unimaginable sog.
My head, though weighed with the weight of St. Michael,
did not fall.
Fine strands of multi-colored gum
suspended it there.
My spirit stopped by my snared torso.
I pulled! I yanked! Rolled it left to right!
It bruised! It softened! It could not free!
The struggle of an Eternity!
An Eternity of pulls! of yanks!
Went back to my head,
St. Michael had sucked dry my brainpan!
Skull!
My skull!
Only skull in heaven!

Went to my legs.
St. Peter was polishing his sandals with my knees!
I pounced upon him!
Pummeled his face in sugar in honey in marmalade!
Under each arm I fled with my legs!
The police of heaven were in hot pursuit!
I hid within the sop of St. Francis.
Gasping in the confectionery of his gentility
I wept, caressing my intimidated legs.

2

They caught me.
They took my legs away.
They sentenced me in the firmament of an ass.
The prison of an Eternity!
An Eternity of labor! of hee-haws!
Burdened with the soiled raiment of saints
I schemed escape.
Lugging ampullae its daily fill
I schemed escape.
I schemed climbing impossible mountains.
I schemed under the Virgin's whip.
I schemed to the sound of celestial joy.
I schemed to the sound of earth,
the wail of infants,
the groans of men,
the thud of coffins.
I schemed escape.
God was busy switching the spheres from hand to hand.
The time had come.
I cracked my jaws.
Broke my legs.
Sagged belly-flat on plow
on pitchfork
on scythe.
My spirit leaked from the wounds.
A whole spirit pooled.

I rose from the carcass of my torment.
I stood in the brink of heaven.
And I swear that Great Territory did quake
when I fell, free.

I Held a Shelley Manuscript

written in Houghton Library, Harvard

My hands did numb to beauty
as they reached into Death and tightened!

O sovereign was my touch
upon the tan-ink's fragile page!

Quickly, my eyes moved quickly,
sought for smell for dust for lace
       for dry hair!

I would have taken the page
breathing in the crime!
For no evidence have I wrung from dreams—
yet what triumph is there in private credence?

Often, in some steep ancestral book,
when I find myself entangled with leopard-apples
       and torched-mushrooms,
my cypressean skein outreaches the recorded age
and I, as though tipping a pitcher of milk,
pour secrecy upon the dying page.

On Pont Neuf

I leave paradise behind me
My paradise squandered fully
What dies dies in beauty
What dies in beauty dies in me—
Alone in this monk cell
I switch money from hand to hand—
With the wrong gate open
I hold a devileye on Red Mountain
—It's a warm evening
An afterrain from noon
Tonight I weep no loveliness
No love!—No love and love!
Cries of love! Cries of no love!
Blasphemies of the loveless!
Harmonies of the loved!
I'd a rope around my neck
A cold shake of music—
O what rang-a-tang crap now meaningless and wet
    beneath one of France's famous men's horses
       do I focus myself?

Poets Hitchhiking on the Highway

Of course I tried to tell him
but he cranked his head
    without an excuse.
I told him the sky chases
    the sun
And he smiled and said:
    'What's the use.'
I was feeling like a demon
    again
So I said: 'But the ocean chases
    the fish.'
This time he laughed
    and said: 'Suppose the
        strawberry were
            pushed into a mountain.'
After that I knew the
    war was on—
So we fought:
He said: 'The apple-cart like a
        broomstick-angel
    snaps & splinters
        old dutch shoes.'
I said: 'Lightning will strike the old oak
    and free the fumes!'
He said: 'Mad street with no name.'
I said: 'Bald killer! Bald killer! Bald killer!'
He said, getting real mad,
    'Firestoves! Gas! Couch!'
I said, only smiling,
    'I know God would turn back his head
    if I sat quietly and thought.'
We ended by melting away,
    hating the air!

Marriage

Should I get married? Should I be good?
Astound the girl next door with my velvet suit and faustus hood?
Don't take her to movies but to cemeteries
tell all about werewolf bathtubs and forked clarinets
then desire her and kiss her and all the preliminaries
and she going just so far and I understanding why
not getting angry saying You must feel! It's beautiful to feel!
Instead take her in my arms lean against an old crooked tombstone
and woo her the entire night the constellations in the sky—

When she introduces me to her parents
back straightened, hair finally combed, strangled by a tie,
should I sit knees together on their 3rd degree sofa
and not ask Where's the bathroom?
How else to feel other than I am,
often thinking Flash Gordon soap—
O how terrible it must be for a young man
seated before a family and the family thinking
We never saw him before! He wants our Mary Lou!
After tea and homemade cookies they ask What do you do for a
                                                                living?

Should I tell them: Would they like me then?
Say All right get married, we're losing a daughter
but we're gaining a son—
And should I then ask Where's the bathroom?

O God, and the wedding! All her family and her friends
and only a handful of mine all scroungy and bearded
just wait to get at the drinks and food—
And the priest! he looking at me as if I masturbated
asking me Do you take this woman for your lawful wedded wife?
And I trembling what to say say Pie Glue!

I kiss the bride all those corny men slapping me on the back
She's all yours, boy! Ha-ha-ha!
And in their eyes you could see some obscene honeymoon going
                                                      on—

Then all that absurd rice and clanky cans and shoes
Niagara Falls! Hordes of us! Husbands! Wives! Flowers!
                                                Chocolates!

All streaming into cozy hotels
All going to do the same thing tonight
The indifferent clerk he knowing what was going to happen
The lobby zombies they knowing what
The whistling elevator man he knowing
The winking bellboy knowing
Everybody knowing! I'd be almost inclined not to do anything!
Stay up all night! Stare that hotel clerk in the eye!
Screaming: I deny honeymoon! I deny honeymoon!
running rampant into those almost climactic suites
yelling Radio belly! Cat shovel!
O I'd live in Niagara forever! in a dark cave beneath the Falls
I'd sit there the Mad Honeymooner
devising ways to break marriages, a scourge of bigamy
a saint of divorce—

But I should get married I should be good
How nice it'd be to come home to her
and sit by the fireplace and she in the kitchen
aproned young and lovely wanting my baby
and so happy about me she burns the roast beef
and comes crying to me and I get up from my big papa chair
saying Christmas teeth! Radiant brains! Apple deaf!
God what a husband I'd make! Yes, I should get married!
So much to do! like sneaking into Mr Jones' house late at night
and cover his golf clubs with 1920 Norwegian books
Like hanging a picture of Rimbaud on the lawnmower
like pasting Tannu Tuva postage stamps all over the picket fence
like when Mrs Kindhead comes to collect for the Community Chest
grab her and tell her There are unfavorable omens in the sky!

And when the mayor comes to get my vote tell him
When are you going to stop people killing whales!
And when the milkman comes leave him a note in the bottle
Penguin dust, bring me penguin dust, I want penguin dust—

Yet if I should get married and it's Connecticut and snow
and she gives birth to a child and I am sleepless, worn,
up for nights, head bowed against a quiet window, the past behind
                                                   me,

finding myself in the most common of situations a trembling man
knowledged with responsibility not twig-smear nor Roman coin
                                                 soup—

O what would that be like!
Surely I'd give it for a nipple a rubber Tacitus
For a rattle a bag of broken Bach records
Tack Della Francesca all over its crib
Sew the Greek alphabet on its bib
And build for its playpen a roofless Parthenon

No, I doubt I'd be that kind of father
not rural not snow no quiet window
but hot smelly tight New York City
seven flights up, roaches and rats in the walls
a fat Reichian wife screeching over potatoes Get a job!
And five nose running brats in love with Batman
And the neighbors all toothless and dry haired
like those hag masses of the 18th century
all wanting to come in and watch TV
The landlord wants his rent
Grocery store Blue Cross Gas & Electric Knights of Columbus
Impossible to lie back and dream Telephone snow, ghost parking—
No! I should not get married I should never get married!
But—imagine If I were married to a beautiful sophisticated woman
tall and pale wearing an elegant black dress and long black gloves
holding a cigarette holder in one hand and a highball in the other

and we lived high up in a penthouse with a huge window
from which we could see all of New York and ever farther on
                                                  clearer days
No, can't imagine myself married to that pleasant prison dream—

O but what about love? I forget love
not that I am incapable of love
it's just that I see love as odd as wearing shoes—
I never wanted to marry a girl who was like my mother
And Ingrid Bergman was always impossible
And there's maybe a girl now but she's already married
And I don't like men and—
but there's got to be somebody!
Because what if I'm 60 years old and not married,
all alone in a furnished room with pee stains on my underwear
and everybody else is married! All the universe married but me!

Ah, yet well I know that were a woman possible as I am possible
then marriage would be possible—
Like SHE in her lonely alien gaud waiting her Egyptian lover
so I wait—bereft of 2,000 years and the bath of life.

Bomb

Budger of history   Brake of time   You   Bomb
Toy of universe   Grandest of all snatched-sky   I cannot hate you
Do I hate the mischievous thunderbolt   the jawbone of an ass
The bumpy club of One Million B.C.   the mace   the flail   the axe
Catapult Da Vinci   tomahawk Cochise   flintlock Kidd   dagger Rathbone
Ah and the sad desperate gun of Verlaine   Pushkin   Dillinger   Bogart
And hath not St. Michael a burning sword   St. George a lance   David a sling
Bomb   you are as cruel as man makes you   and you're no crueller than cancer
All man hates you   they'd rather die by car-crash   lightning   drowning
Falling off a roof   electric-chair   heart-attack   old age   old age   O Bomb
They'd rather die by anything but you   Death's finger is free-lance
Not up to man whether you boom or not   Death has long since distributed its
categorical blue   I sing thee Bomb   Death's extravagance   Death's jubilee
Gem of Death's supremest blue   The flyer will crash   his death will differ
with the climber who'll fall   To die by cobra is not to die by bad pork
Some die by swamp   some by sea   and some by the bushy-haired man in the night
O there are deaths like witches of Arc   Scarey deaths like Boris Karloff
No-feeling deaths like birth-death   sadless deaths like old pain Bowery
Abandoned deaths   like Capital Punishment   stately deaths like senators
And unthinkable deaths like Harpo Marx   girls on Vogue covers   my own
I do not know just how horrible Bombdeath is   I can only imagine
Yet no other death I know has so laughable a preview   I scope
a city   New York City   streaming   starkeyed   subway shelter
Scores and scores   A fumble of humanity   High heels bend
Hats whelming away   Youth forgetting their combs
Ladies not knowing what to do   with their shopping bags
Unperturbed gum machines   Yet dangerous 3rd rail
Ritz Brothers   from the Bronx   caught in the A train
The smiling Schenley poster will always smile
Impish Death   Satyr Bomb   Bombdeath
Turtles exploding over Istanbul
The jaguar's flying foot
soon to sink in arctic snow
Penguins plunged against the Sphinx
The top of the Empire State

arrowed in a broccoli field in Sicily
Eiffel shaped like a C in Magnolia Gardens
St. Sophia peeling over Sudan
O athletic Death   Sportive Bomb
The temples of ancient times
their grand ruin ceased
Electrons   Protons   Neutrons
gathering Hesperean hair
walking the dolorous golf of Arcady
joining marble helmsmen
entering the final amphitheater
with a hymnody feeling of all Troys
heralding cypressean torches
racing plumes and banners
yet knowing Homer with a step of grace
Lo the visiting team of Present
the home team of Past
Lyre and tuba together joined
Hark the hotdog soda olive grape
gala galaxy robed and uniformed
commissary   O the happy stands
Ethereal root and cheer and boo
The billioned all-time attendance
The Zeusian pandemonium
Hermes racing Owens
the Spitball of Buddha
Christ striking out
Luther stealing third
Planetarium Death   Hosannah Bomb
Gush the final rose   O Spring Bomb
Come with thy gown of dynamite green
unmenace Nature's inviolate eye
Before you the wimpled Past
behind you the hallooing Future   O Bomb
Bound in the grassy clarion air
like the fox of the tally-ho
thy field the universe thy hedge the geo
Leap Bomb   bound Bomb   frolic zig and zag
The stars a swarm of bees in thy binging bag
Stick angels on your jubilee feet

wheels of rainlight on your bunky seat
You are due and behold you are due
and the heavens are with you
hosannah incalescent glorious liaison
BOMB O havoc antiphony molten cleft BOOM
Bomb mark infinity a sudden furnace
spread thy multitudinous encompassed Sweep
set forth awful agenda
Carrion stars   charnel planets   carcass elements
Corpse the universe   tee-hee finger-in-the-mouth hop
over its long long dead Nor
From thy nimbled matted spastic eye
exhaust deluges of celestial ghouls
From thy appellational womb
spew birth-gusts of great worms
Rip open your belly Bomb
from your belly outflock vulturic salutations
Battle forth your spangled hyena finger stumps
along the brink of Paradise
O Bomb   O final Pied Piper
both sun and firefly behind your shock waltz
God abandoned mock-nude
beneath His thin false-talc'd apocalypse
He cannot hear thy flute's
happy-the-day profanations
He is spilled deaf into the Silencer's warty ear
His Kingdom an eternity of crude wax
Clogged clarions untrumpet Him
Sealed angels unsing Him
A thunderless God   A dead God
O Bomb   thy BOOM His tomb
That I lean forward on a desk of science
an astrologer dabbling in dragon prose
half-smart about wars   bombs   especially bombs
That I am unable to hate what is necessary to love
That I can't exist in a world that consents
a child in a park   a man dying in an electric-chair
That I am able to laugh at all things
all that I know and do not know   thus to conceal my pain

That I say I am a poet and therefore love all man
knowing my words to be the acquainted prophecy of all men
and my unwords no less an acquaintanceship
That I am manifold
a man pursuing the big lies of gold
or a poet roaming in bright ashes
or that which I imagine myself to be
a shark-toothed sleep   a man-eater of dreams
I need not then be all-smart about bombs
Happily so   for if I felt bombs were caterpillars
I'd doubt not they'd become butterflies
There is a hell for bombs
They're there   I see them there
They sit in bits and sing songs
mostly German songs
and two very long American songs
and they wish there were more songs
especially Russian and Chinese songs
and some more very long American songs
Poor little Bomb that'll never be
an Eskimo song   I love thee
I want to put a lollipop
in thy furcal mouth
A wig of Goldilocks on thy baldy bean
and have you skip with me Hansel and Gretel
along the Hollywoodian screen
O Bomb in which all lovely things
moral and physical anxiously participate
O fairyflake plucked from the
grandest universe tree
O piece of heaven which gives
both mountain and anthill a sun
I am standing before your fantastic lily door
I bring you Midgardian roses   Arcadian musk
Reputed cosmetics from the girls of heaven
Welcome me   fear not thy opened door
nor thy cold ghost's grey memory
nor the pimps of indefinite weather
their cruel terrestrial thaw

Oppenheimer is seated
in the dark pocket of Light
Fermi is dry in Death's Mozambique
Einstein his mythmouth
a barnacled wreath on the moon-squid's head
Let me in   Bomb   rise from that pregnant-rat corner
nor fear the raised-broom nations of the world
O Bomb I love you
I want to kiss your clank   eat your boom
You are a paean   an acme of scream
a lyric hat of Mister Thunder
O resound thy tanky knees
BOOM   BOOM   BOOM   BOOM   BOOM
BOOM ye skies and BOOM ye suns
BOOM BOOM ye moons   ye stars BOOM
nights ye BOOM   ye days ye BOOM
BOOM BOOM ye winds   ye clouds ye rains
go BANG ye lakes   ye oceans BING
Barracuda BOOM and cougar BOOM
Ubangi BANG   orangoutang
BING BANG BONG BOOM   bee bear baboon
ye BANG ye BONG ye BING
the tail the fin the wing
Yes   Yes   into our midst a bomb will fall
Flowers will leap in joy their roots aching
Fields will kneel proud beneath the halleluyahs of the wind
Pinkbombs will blossom   Elkbombs will perk their ears
Ah many a bomb that day will awe the bird a gentle look
Yet   not enough to say a bomb will fall
or even contend celestial fire goes out
Know that the earth will madonna the Bomb
that in the hearts of men to come more bombs will be born
magisterial bombs wrapped in ermine   all beautiful
and they'll sit plunk on earth's grumpy empires
fierce with moustaches of gold

*

* *

She Doesn't Know He Thinks He's God

He is God
Jim Blaze is God
He stands by the window smiling
watching a child walk by
'I am God!' he smiles.   He knows

His wife taps him on the shoulder
'Jim the baby is sick will die
His fever is up.   Get a doctor.'

Jim Blaze stands as though he were dead
with the health and freshness of life
exaggerated in his deathness
He stands a man stunned with the realization
that he's God.   He is God!

His wife pleads screams stamps the floor
pounds her fists against the wall
'Jim the baby will die!'

Dream of a Baseball Star

I dreamed Ted Williams
leaning at night
against the Eiffel Tower, weeping.

He was in uniform
and his bat lay at his feet
—knotted and twiggy.

'Randall Jarrell says you're a poet!' I cried.
'So do I! I say you're a poet!

He picked up his bat with blown hands;
stood there astraddle as he would in the batter's box,
and laughed! flinging his schoolboy wrath
toward some invisible pitcher's mound
—waiting the pitch all the way from heaven.

It came; hundreds came! all afire!
He swung and swung and swung and connected not one
sinker curve hook or right-down-the-middle.
A hundred strikes!
The umpire dressed in strange attire
thundered his judgment: YOU'RE OUT!
And the phantom crowd's horrific boo
dispersed the gargoyles from Notre Dame.

And I screamed in my dream:
God! throw thy merciful pitch!
Herald the crack of bats!

Hooray the sharp liner to left!
Yea the double, the triple!
Hosannah the home run!

DREAM of a Baseball Star
Gregory Corso

Giant Turtle

from a Walt Disney film

You rise from the sea an agony of sea
Night in the moonlight you slow the shore
Behind you webbed-tracks mark your ordeal
An hour   in an hour you cease your slow
Hind legs now digging   digging the sand the damp the sand
The moon brightens   the sea calms
Your mouth pumping   your eyes thickly tearing
You create a tremendous hole   you fall flat
Exhaust   sigh   strain
Eggs   eggs   eggs   eggs   eggs   eggs   eggs   eggs   eggs
Eggs   eggs   eggs   eggs   egg   egg   egg
Heave   exhaust   sigh   flat
Your wet womb speckled with sand   you turn slow
Slow you cover the hole the eggs slow   slow
You cease your slow
Dawn
And you plop in the sea like a big rock

A Dreamed Realization

The carrion-eater's nobility calls back from God;
Never was a carrion-eater *first* a carrion-eater—
Back there in God creatures sat like stone
—no light in their various eyes.

Life. It was Life jabbed a spoon in their mouths.
Crow jackal hyena vulture worm woke to necessity
—dipping into Death like a soup.

Paranoia in Crete

Damned Minoan crevices, that I clog them up!
Plaster myself away from everything, all that out there!
Just sit here, knees up, amid amphora and aloe,
reading lusty potsherd, gobbling figs, needing no one—
Mine the true labyrinth, it is my soul, Theseus;
try a ball of string in *that!*

Thrones descended by kings are ascended by ruin;
upon no singular breast do I rest my head of mythologies;
no footman seat, no regnant couch, enough this pillowy cave—
O Zeus! I was such a king able to mobilize everything!
A king advised by oraclry his aulic valets imperium;
not kingsmen, nor my sons, that pederast Miletus;
that hot-shot Rhadamanthys, his nine year cave advocacy—
And my wife! that wood-cow brothel!

Clog! Clog! Clog! Stuff-up the cracks!
They'd like to dump me in a miserable nymph's bubbling brake!
Vise my feet in the River-god's mouth!
Perplex my head with Naiads!
Set Eros on me, that sequesterer of mortal vanity!
O Calypso's green-fluid boudoir is tearing me to pieces!
Plaster! Plaster! Stay the Aegean tide! Blot out Athens!

I survey the hunched bull, the twin headless lions,
one more crevice to go, and lo!
I forfeit the Echinadian Isles—

Clown

1

Laughter dies long after jest
The joker smiles no joke
A clown in a grave
Pranksters weep in Purgatory
Laughter dies long after jest
Joy
Bella, the memory of the heart
Yet the face is a joker smiling no joke

2

Like the jester who blew out candles
tip-toeing in toe-bell feet
that his master dream victories
—so I creep and blow
that the cat and canary sleep.

I've no plumed helmet, no blue-white raiment;
and no jester of-old comes wish me on.
I myself am my own happy fool.

As there are no fields for me to dedragon
—impossible to kneel before ladies
and kiss their flowery gowns.
I can only walk up and down hands behind my back
dreaming dungeons and spikes and squeaking racks.

For commoners, I put things on my nose
and tip-toe with the grace of gold.
For those I love I sit sad by stained glass
—all my face the mystery of some joke.
And for God I am ready with a mouthful of penguins.

I lock myself away!
I wash myrtle-birds in the sink.
Yes, I myself am my own happy fool
—stale with dreamless jokes.

Do I care? Yes I care. I want to make laugh.
O if only I were a winding toy
or just a winter bunny
        in a huge imbecile's pie.

I know laughter! I know lots of laughter!
Yet all I do is walk up and down hands behind back
dreaming dungeons spikes and squeaking racks.

3

And why do they say be a man, not a clown?
And what is it like to be a man?
I can joke like a saint for my need,
give in return for a goose-leg, a glow;
I need never know this joy I grease through life
or claim on woe substantial diet.
Fat if I want to be fat!
So easy to ice one's humor
—to fan the sun.

It is time for the idiot
to pose a grin and foot on the dead lion
(the embodiment of the clownless man)—
Time to grow a mustache; suck gin;
and win the hard-to-get lady.
Time to return from star trek
and scrub the earth.

Where am I in wilderness?
What creature bore my bones to this?
Here is no Eden—this is my store:
Rooms! Rooms! Electric lights!
A giant ocean on each shore.

Am I the man to jack-in-the-box
each misfortune of man, be it sickness
death or simply an unhappiness?
That man? That old clown
        with bent hat and tubed beard?
That looney tearfully recalling
        his rainbow ball?

No! Boot the jack of clubs into devildom!
Turn somersaults in the circus-coffin!
Mr. Death has the hero by the balls!

—I can commemorate black laughter, too.

                    4

I still don't know if the clown should die;
there's yet the black greyhound, the lioned battle axe;
the champ of heaven leaning against a cloud
        with crossed feet;
and the doomed myth
        centered in man war.

If there were no clown
but demoned whiskers shaking pale blue flowers;
if there were no smile
no climb of cherubim with lute and horn
no silvery chest, no suncast jug, no basin for swans,
not the delicate forge itself;
I doubt the reward of Paradise
to be a place where happy old friends meet.

If the clown were dead
the month of August would be weighed
        with sacks of sour wheat.
Dead the clown, there'd be havoc!
The angel's jeweled apse
        would collide
        and smash a ray of doves!

Fauns would lay waste the wood
        with faun-chewed babes!
Oily melancholy fits the black boot
now that the clown thinks to die.
Men the size of islands
        sink their joy in the helpless protect of Death.

O the whole tragedy! the weight of it!
with complaints to laughter not come—
Tickle then the clown to sleep for sleep he needs;
glum days poor America bares—
Old America could tell of laughter often as clowns tell—
Ben Franklin, W. C. Fields, Chaplin, the fat of joy!
Their happy light is forged phalanx, charge!

Snakes search the skies for flying rabbits;
monkies draft jackels—is the clown dead?
I grieve to futures a fishy grin,
for as I am I gloom of history.
A comical corruption! Death's indeathity!
The clocked tower's scythed crime
bodes sorrow and the life of man equal time.

                5

Proud boastful buffoon! at full your fancies
swing swift youngyear to oldyear.

Is it for Death you rend black profit,
this meagre vanity deserved me?

It is life has flawed my gentle song;

sad intelligence examples my secret rich behavior,
o foremost physician at my dying side.

Good tricker! I distinguish your twisted floors
your ribboned furniture, your anguished doors.

Ho! you good mad pest of joy!
I won't stab your eyes with night,

or place a watchman's apey grapple
to nab you with his moral tickle.

You are not laughable
You have never been laughable
You have always been you, clown!
—a graft of lunacy on heaven's diadem.

Yet I die in thee;
fill your heart my tomb—

Forgive me, lovely one;
o there's that in me wishes each laugh
would knit an eternity of hilarity!

No, I shan't crowd your brainy grave;
it's enough I climb your jolly ladder
and have planets kick dust in my eyes.

Don't despair kind child of joy,
you'll get to God
and ease His dreadful tightrope.

6

The punches of winter knocked out a herd of deer.
Winter left the wood like a plate of chicken bones.
The naked clown shivers by the snowy brook;
the sleeping bear wakes to mock his bony blue legs.
Hold on, clown!
Every stone is cosmos;
every tree made of laughter stuff.
Paint wide your mouth white!
With elm leaves make fake ears!
Redden your nose with lizards!
Be ready!

Spring will soon step out from behind a tree
    like Eve from the side of Adam.

Tang-a-lang boom! Fife feef! Toot!
Spring welcomed by Barnum parade clears jammed melancholy
—traffic of a laughless age.
Mothers break their backs getting out winter babies.
Children climb daringly
    and sit with shirtsleeves on the shoulders of statues.
Cherry blossoms swell joy in the hearts of the old.
Girls skip, boys gather, dogs bound, cats leap—
Spring!
Good to go to the East River
and sit before Brooklyn
    with fresh knowledge of Hesiod on farming;
good to be intent on Alcman's *Maiden Song;*
sit good for hours re-learning
    the craft of classical verse—
Welcome Epinikian ode!

Yo! Yo! Myths of calamity
    announce heat heat by noonlight
    grains and berry-bees!
Elves bring handfuls of Spring
    to the dying winter king;
the old Crinch berry poisoned
    will soon be dead
    will soon be dead.

I knew you'd come, wild architect!
It's you I want; o heartily I laugh!
Why continue to bother about the profane ransom of Rome
when there's you? let the Turks and the missing noses of Greece
roil on the bottom of the Ottoman's grease pot.

Yo! God! Go ye snowdogs and fumigations!
Unlike the fauns on the banks of the Tiber
there's nursery for this age's cloven feet.

Winter, that I've been your clown;
that I've read your beady scripture
—I hold no grudge.
My joy could never wedge free
        from sorrow's old crack.

7

To the unicorn cling, failing
unlaughable lover of man; your red nose
is antideath—

A jerk of March you are—
Born in mockery, o that crazy month!
But born in mockery like all men
        from the womby head of a cheapskate,
a stingy creep who got great kicks
out of not telling you when and how and why life.

Enough. To the unicorn.
The clown's allowance of joy to man is useless.
Man is glued to sorrow and there is no escape.
All your slapstick gold . . . useless.

Go! cling to the unicorn with faked ears and tufted hats
—you'll never shake Death's laughter of mercy, poor nut!

Clown!
Homeless clown in Serious!

8

Of course the unicorn will be killed
so don't think your red nose
your flabber mouth
your million dollar laugh won't.

Of course the circus will mourn.
The fat lady they'll mourn less.

You made kids laugh to make money
so don't think you're a golden clown.
The time you cursed an acrobat
the time you refused a beggar
the time you cried.

Ah, it's not the circus clown I sing;
not the tumbling midge before the conqueror
        made to dance before horses,
not the Joker whose arsenal teeth
        explosively haw-haws out of jams;
no, nor is it the Tricker in whose hand the rope ends.

                9

The comedy gone mad!
Poor clown, the weather of sorrow.

The clown's house FOR SALE!
        Crying bricks and porch
        Rotting door and windows
        and neat slopes of buttercups.

This night the finished clown
his stumps flash on gypsy caravan.
The swinging lantern objects his leaving home.
He's a phantom to crystal;
to ears he's hairy batter;
the hag's future glimpse
scarce allows him identity.
The moon garments a cloud;
the last wagon baits two trees;
he catches his ruffled neck
—whoa!,his goopy scent!
Birds gulp his amulets baubles and trinklets.

The clown is dead!
Pass along the highways of 1959—all clowns are dead!
See the great dumps of them swarmed by seagulls;

their tufted hats frayed
their face noses and ears smoldering
their polka-dot coveralls darkening
    underneath the sun-fairy's final nighthorn.

The helly ringmaster cracks his whip!
The circus's great mercy shoots fire!
Acrobats gnaw their wires!
Skeletal apes twist meatless bananas!
The lion trainer's bony jaw
    clanks on the lion's bony jaw!
Hotdogs and coca cola for the charnel!
Elephant trickdust on the purgative scale!
Fifty shrouded clowns pile out
    from a tiny tomb.

10

But
I am an always clown
and need not make grammatic
    Death's diameter.
Death, like a monkey's tail,
wraps down spirally on a rising,
    ever rising pole.

How to climb and sit on the turret
away from the breath of the sick
away from the souls who sleep
    in Death's cylindrical kick—
Ah,
    this surfeit of charlatanry
will never leave my organic pyx
    thank God

The Sacré-Coeur Café

The fierce girls in the Sacré-Coeur Café
bang their wines on the table
screaming Danton triumphed having denied liberty
While the garçon demands Murat triumph on all that triumphs.
The bombed Algerians observe each others' burning teeth.
A scarey café the Sacré-Coeur Café.
The proprietors are like the proprietors in Les Misérables.
Always making me feel like Jean Valjean when I go there.
Thank God I've no sack of silver no yellow ticket to show.
But that's why I go there an ex-convict with no lodgings
sitting in a wooden corner eating black bread
waiting for little Cosette—the size of eternity.
Wait there that I follow her out into the night
that I might carry her water buckets
buy her a huge glorious doll
and take her far away
that she love me
that I carry her lover on my back through sewers
that I old and grey die at their wedding table.
Ah but there are plastic tables in the Sacré-Coeur Café.
The fierce girls all work in the Post Office.
The proprietors have no Cosette but a big fat son
who sits dunking croissants.
And the Algerians
they don't go to the Sacré-Coeur Café.

Mortal Infliction

I think of Polyphemus bellowing his lowly woe
seated high on a cliff
sun-tight legs dangling into the sea
his fumbling hands grappling his burnt eye
And I think he will remain like that
because it's impossible for him to die—-

Ulysses is dead
by now he's dead
And how wise was he
who blinded a thing of immortality?

From Another Room

Dumb genius blows
feeble breath into my windowless room
He—the sagacious mute
rap-tapping a code of doom
—the drunkard punched the wall to have his storm!
Through the crack! Through the crack!
My feast was in the easy blood that flowed.

Power

for Allen Ginsberg

We are the imitation of Power
Every man is to be doubted
There is no mouth no eye no nose no ear no hand enough
The senses are insufficient
You need Power to dispel light
Not the closing of an eye

Since I observe memory and dream
And not the images of the moment
I am become more vivid
And need not open the eye to see
With me light is always light
How powerful I am to imagine darkness!

Since I depend on heroes for opinion and acceptance
I live by proper truth and error
SHAZAM!
O but how sad is Ted Williams   gypped and chiseled
All alone in center field
Let me be your wise Buck Rogers!

Since I contradict the real with the unreal
Nothing is so unjust as impossibility
Outstepping myself as a man in Azerbaijan
I forge a rocket lion
And with a heart of wooing mathematics soar to passion a planet

O but there are times SHAZAM is not enough
There is a brutality in the rabbit
That leads the way to Paradise—far from God!
There is a cruelness in the fawn
Its tiger-elegance gnawing clover to the bone

I am a creature of Power
With me there is no ferocity
I am fair   careful   wise and laughable
I storm a career of love for myself
I am powerful humancy in search of compassion
My Power craves love   Beware my Power!

Know my Power
I resemble fifty miles of Power
I cut my fingernails with a red Power
In buses I stand on huge volumes of Spanish Power
The girl I love is like a goat splashing golden cream Power
Throughout the Spring I carried no Power

But my mission is outrageous!
I am here to tell you various failures of God
The unreasonableness of God
There is something unfair about this
It is not God that has made Power unbearable   it is Love
Love of Influence   Industry   Firearms   Protection
Man protected by man from man   this is Love
Good has no meaning and Sympathy no message   this is Love
THINK signs will never give way to DREAM signs   this is Love
We are ready to fight with howitzers!   this is Love
This has never been my Love
Thank God my Power

Who am I that sing of Power
Am I the stiff arm of Nicaragua
Do I wear green and red in Chrysler squads
Do I hate my people
What about the taxes
Do they forgive me their taxes
Am I to be shot at the racetrack—do they plot now
My monument of sculptured horses is white beneath the moon!

Am I Don Pancho Magnifico Pulque no longer a Power?
No I do not sing of dictatorial Power
The hail of dictatorship is symbolic of awful Power
In my room I have gathered enough gasoline and evidence
To allow dictators inexhaustible Power

I *Ave* no particular Power but that of Life
Nor yet condemn fully any form of Power but that of Death
The inauguration of Death is an absurd Power
Life is the supreme Power
Whoever hurts Life is a penny candy in the confectionary of Power
Whoever complains about Life is a dazzling monster in the zoo of
                                                    Power

The lovers of Life are deserved of Power's trophy
They need not jump Power's olympics nor prove pilgrimage
Each man is a happy spy of Power in the realm of Weakness

Power
What is Power
A hat is Power
The world is Power
Being afraid is Power
What is poetry when there is no Power
Poetry is powerless when there is no Power
Standing on a street corner waiting for no one is Power
The angel is not as powerful as looking and then not looking
Will Power make me mean and unforgettable?

Power is underpowered
Power is what is happening
Power is without body or spirit
Power is sadly fundamental
Power is attained by Weakness
Diesels do not explain Power
In Power there is no destruction
Power is not to be dropped by a plane

A thirst for Power is drinking sand
I want no song Power
I want no dream Power
I want no driven-car Power
I want I want I want Power!

Power is without compensation
Angels of Power come down with cups of vengeance
They are demanding compensation
People! where is your Power
The angels of Power are coming down with their cups!

I am the ambassador of Power
I walk through tunnels of fear
With portfolios of Power under my arm
Look at me
The appearance of Power is there
I have come to survey your store of Power—where is it
Is it in your heart your purse
Is it beneath your kitchen sink
Beautiful people I remember your Power
I have not forgotten you in the snows of Bavaria
Skiing down on the sleeping villages with flares and carbines
I have not forgotten you rubbing your greasy hands on aircraft
Singing your obscene names on blockbusters
No! I have not forgotten the bazooka you decked with palm
Fastened on the shoulder of a black man
Aimed at a tankful of Aryans
Nor have I forgotten the grenade
The fear and emergency it spread
Throughout your brother's trench
You are Power beautiful people

In a playground where I write this poem feeling shot in the back
Wanting to change the old meaning of Power
Wanting to give it new meaning my meaning
I drop my unusual head dumb to the true joy of being good

And I wonder myself now powerless
Staggering back to the feeble boys of my youth
Are they now lesser men in the factories of universe
Are they there compressing the air
Pumping their bully profanities through long leafy tubes
I see them perched high on the shelves of God
Outpecking this offered hemisphere like a crumb—
O God! what uttered curse ushers me to them
Like a prisoner of war . . .
Be those ominous creaks of eternity their sad march?

How powerless I am in playgrounds
Swings like witches woosh about me
Sliding ponds like dinosaur tongues down to my unusual feet
To have me walk in the street would be *both* unusual

                                                    —1956

1958—
Power is still with me! Who got me hung on Power?
Am I stuffed in the grizzly maw of Power's hopped-up wheel
Will I always be like this   head in   legs out
Like one of Ulysses' men in the mouth of Polyphemus
Am I the Power drag? Me   the Power head?
Just what Power am I for anyway!
The seized bee in a glaze of honey Power—
The spider in the center of its polar veil
With a fly-from-another-world Power—
Good noon nap on adoration lap with all cozy cruelty Power—
Towering melt like an avalanche of glass never ending chirring

                                                    Power—

Stooped and hushed Chronicleleer of Spenserian gauderies
Is surely maybe my Power—
Whenever I play the fiery lyre with cold-fingered minstrelry
A luscious Power gives me a heavened consequence good as

                                                    sunlight—

Awful blank acreage once made pastoral by myths ·
Now abandoned to mankind's honest yet hopeless
Anthemion-elixir is in need of my Power—
But the Power I have I built with my own help!
That bad wolf approach in dim-divine disguise Power
All mine! All illumination sheep Power!
That woodsy savant fetch-eyed scarce perspective from
Balm-volumed epics that prouds shy fantasy my Power!
That hand-grenade humor dropped down the hatch
Of an armoured suit my proposed bit come doomsday Power!
O joy to my human sparkle Power!
Joy to its march down the street!
Ha! The envy of diamonds in the windows!
The child of Power is laughter!

October you fat month of gloom and poetry
It's no longer your melodious graveyard air
Your night-yanked cypresses
Your lovely dead moon
It is October of me! My Power!
Alive with a joy a sparkle a laugh
That drops my woe and all woe to the floor
Like a shot spy

Army

Thrice I've seen the two-gunned ghost of Patton
waxing wars in the backroom   whitehaired and mad
his fat thumbs pressing violence with schoolboy gaud.
He hates God he has alchemy cannons aimed at Him!
Badgered angels (wine-soaked rags) slaughtered by his orders
by his battalions of exorbitant drunks
hang (not as sweet Alexander would have it hang)
like rags in the bombblotched air of God.
Yet . . . those who die most courteous
do become the dreadful applause in any great decline.
Remember,
trembling aristocracies   doomed
laughed to slay flies.

I think of war mythical wars
flowing from the wrinkled mouths of bards
wars that defile tears
uplift horrible iniquities
plunge complaints in noble speech
turn white the infant hair of the world
wars that go mad
that banish the leaking ox   the stuck pig   the pinned swan
wars that drink blackberries
wars that pee behind the hideous shack of Farm
wars wars wars
war: A blessed hour
stole from the heaven of God.

I left the imagination army
stricken by the penitential muster
over my shoulder a swollen gun—
I made my way to instant wars
my medals were laughing faces
in my hand I held a diploma of Rifle

Ah what war next? I stood on the threshold
my army-gloved hand, its woeful knock,
provoked the door of Peace;
Athene requests my unbecoming.

I stepped upon an old bombardment
my path pyloned by dark meditative Generals.
'So!' I cried, 'So this is the sadness of Generals!'
I sat awhile in the arms of Eisenhower and slept
and dreamed a great bomb had died,
its death rattle made Stentor
in the breast of my human bed.

I ran down the bombarded fetch of war
North of Rzhev
in the bend of the Don
on the hump of Stalingrad
outrunning the German General Staff
fled from Rostov (confused)
the only exit the Kerch Straits
now where? now where?
Beyond the Crimea
—a lonely dark wet wicker basket.
O the basins of the Don
the Volga
the great bend of the Don
Generals Vatutin Golikov Kuznetsov
Leliushenko
How can I love the Army?
Doves honk it wicked!
Nothing I know wishes a young man die
(perhaps Army)
One concise bullet aimed at the heart
can never separate youth from youth
(perhaps Army can)
Even with all its helmets
who can love the Army?
(Army)

Army walks the battlefield and does not retreat
Army kneels before the boys who fell and
revels in the fragrance of their gunpowdered mouths
Army likes to hieroglyph the ground
with fragments of lyric youth.
How can I love the Army?

From foxhole illusion where I sit
secretly drawing pictures of my mother
I know I am but a stupid boy waiting to be shot
Yet no thing I know in man wishes me die.

They said shoot the young boy and I did.
I would like to have shot him at a distance
They had me put the pistol to the back of his head
I cried
but the army summoned the brass band
(its prestige and morale supply)
and soon my sobs became song.

That war gives me chance
to breathe air appreciatively
          is wonderful
That I may die with all my beautiful hair
          is not forbidden
That I no longer dream of Jane or my cats
but of Flying Fortresses
          is forgivable
That I can tear the faces of youth
That I can char their heads
That I can give them smoking knees
That I can
Army you dirty rotten—O my heart!
I know you'd like me to make friends
with my fellow soldiers
but I'll not!
Tonight when attack screams us back into infancy
I'd not like to hear them bullet-torn tell me:
'Death is a consuming blackness'   how dull!

I've heard that in all your other wars.
How sad the first buddy I took by the hand in death
who, in words of blood, said:
'That a soldier can't die a unique death is lamentable.'

Rommel leads Hollywood across the Sahara
Montgomery flees!
Zhukov clumps like the baths of Caracalla into Berlin
Rundstedt hides in the bombed opera house
his shiny boots gathering dust in the back room of Gigli
Guderian examines with tears in his drooping swastika eyes
Ukrainian pitchfork wounds in his mistress tanks
Eisenhower yanks out appendix
thus to lead healthy wealthy and wise the whole shebang!
And miles and miles away Shades MacArthur
wets his knees in tropic water
the mangled children of Buddha floating pass his eagled belly
                                                                                          button.

Battalions! Platoons! Garrisons!
In everywhere they go they war
hand in hand
their promises mutual
their hearts faulty
In everywhere they go they kill
some carry diaries
some, poems
everyone reads a sacred prayer
Army's sacred prayer
Holy be to Papa Patton who leads us
into the poolrooms and brothels of War!
Holy be to Papa Patton, he'd never fight Nebuchadnezzar!
He leads us fatherly martherly gartherly into
Death! Death! Death! Death! Death!
Bullets in our blue eyes, holy be to Patton!
Grenades in our bellies, Patton!
Tanks over our bright blond hair!
O Harpo Death and thy clanking harp, hear!
Holy be to Patton he gives hills to Death!
Army! Army! Army! Army!

1959

Uncomprising year—I see no meaning to life.
Though this abled self is here nonetheless,
either in trade gold or grammaticness,
I drop the wheelwright's simple principle—
Why weave the garland? Why ring the bell?

Penurious butchery these notoriously human years,
these confident births these lucid deaths these years.
Dream's flesh blood reals down life's mystery—
there is no mystery.
Cold history knows no dynastic Atlantis.
The habitual myth has an eagerness to quit.

No meaning to life can be found in this holy language
nor beyond the lyrical fabricator's inescapable theme
be found the loathed find—there is nothing to find.

Multitudinous deathplot! O this poor synod—
Hopers and seekers paroling meaning to meaning,
annexing what might be meaningful, what might be meaningless.

Repeated nightmare, lachrymae lachrymae—
a fire behind a grotto, a thick fog, shredded masts,
the nets heaved—and the indescribable monster netted.
Who was it told that red flesh hose be still?
For one with smooth hands did with pincers
snip the snout—It died like a yawn.
And when the liver sack was yanked
I could not follow it to the pan.

I could not follow it to the pan—
I woke to the reality of cars; Oh
the dreadful privilege of that vision!
Not one antique faction remained;

Egypt, Rome, Greece,
and all such pedigree dreams fled.
Cars are real! Eternity is done.
The threat of Nothingness renews.
I touch the untouched.
I rank the rose militant.
Deny, I deny the tastes and habits of the age.
I am its punk debauché. . . . A fierce lampoon
seeking to inherit what is necessary to forfeit.

Lies! Lies! Lies! I lie, you lie, we all lie!
There is no us, there is no world, there is no universe,
there is no life, no death, no nothing—all is meaningless,
and this too is a lie—O damned 1959!
Must I dry my inspiration in this sad concept?
Delineate my entire stratagem?
Must I settle into phantomness
and not say I understand things better than God?

From **LONG LIVE MAN**

Man

prologue to what was to be a long long poem

The good scope of him is history, old and ironic;
Not modern history, unfulfilled and blurred—
Bleak damp fierce thunderous lightning days;
Poor caveman, so scared of the outside,
So afeared of its power and beauty,
Created a limit, and called that limit God—
Cell, fish, apeman, Adam;
How was the first man born?
And why has he ceased being born that way?

Air his fuel, will his engine, legs his wheels,
Eyes the steer, ears the alert;
He could not fly, but now he does—
The nails hair teeth bones blood
All in communion with the flesh;
The heart that feels all things in life
And lastly feels in death;
The hands in looks and action are masterful;
The eyes the eyes;
The penis is a magic wand,
The womb greater than Spring—

I do not know if he be Adam's heir
Or kin to ape,
No man knows; what a good driving mystery—
I can imagine a soul, the soul leaving the body,
The body feeding death, death simply a hygiene;
I can wonder the world the factory of the soul,
The soul putting on a body like a workman's coveralls,
Building, unbuilding, rebuilding.
That man can *think* soul is a great strange wonderful thing—

In the beginning was the word; man has spoken—
The Jews, the Greeks; chaos groping behind;
Exalted dignity sings; the blind angel's cithara
Twanged no chain-reaction that World War be the Trojan War,
Not with the goddess Eris denied a wedding seat;
No praise of man in my war, wars have lost their legendariness—
The Bible sings man in all his glory;
Great Jew, man is hard stem of you,
Was you first spoke love, O noble survivor;
The Greeks are gone, the Egyptians have all but vanished;
Your testament yet holds—

The fall of man stands a lie before Beethoven,
A truth before Hitler—
Man is the victory of life,
And Christ be the victory of man—
King of the universe is man, creator of gods;
He knows no thing other than himself
And he knows himself the best he can;
He exists as a being of nature
And sustains all things in being;
His dream can go beyond existence—
Greater the rose?
The simple bee does not think so;
When man sings birds humble into piety;
What history can the whale empire sing?
What genius ant dare break from anthood
As can man from manhood?
King Agamemnon! Mortal man!
Ah, immortality—

ttle mozart has
where to go . . . . .

Dear Girl

With people conformed
Away from pre-raphaelite furniture
With no promise but that of Japanese sparsity
I take up house
Ready to eat with you and sleep with you

But when the conquered spirit breaks free
And indicates a new light
Who'll take care of the cats?

Writ When I Found Out His Was an Unmarked Grave

Children children don't you know
Mozart has no where to go
This is so
Though graves be many
He hasn't any

Happening on a German Train

From a fast-moving train window
on my way to King Ludwig's castle
I watched past a recurrence of trees
a white bird fly straight and low;
how extraordinary how it kept
up to the speed of the train
—then suddenly I heard two loud pops
resound in the sky;
the bird disappeared.
The train slowed to a stop
and everyone looked out the windows,
"There it is! There!"
Down at an angle
so smooth so sleek so silent
a white American jet fighter plane
CRASHBOOM and billows of orange.

*Note: The two pop sounds having been the release of the ejector seat which
parachuted the pilot to safety.*

European Thoughts—1959

If there was never a home to go to
there was always a home not to go to
Well I know when a child as a runaway
I slept on the subway
and it would always stop
at the station where the home I ran from was
That was the bitterest sorrow oh it was

How would it be if I
ran up to every man I encountered
and with a big happy smile said:
"Isn't everything great!"
Or ran into a crowded restaurant and yelled:
"Bon appétit!"

When the ladies of Germany at war's end
stood amid the rubble wondering their men
and the old poked in the rubble for their homes again
did they not see the many-legged swastika
nudge like a bug under the rubble
pregnant with peace?
It seems German children were not spared
fifteen years later, today,
the sorrow of that rubble.
There are other things written on walls
Can Merde shock more than 卐 ?
And things like U S GO HOME
ALGERIA IS FRENCH or REMEMBER HUNGARY
are they really worse than MERDE?
And Greece was a marvelous country
but of course I was not marvelous in it
because man is made to suffer in a happy place
when he has been happy all too happy
in an insufferable place.

The Love of Two Seasons

When once in wildhood times
I'd aerial laughter my mischief

When once she opened her arms
And held me with excited tenderness

I laughed
She laughed

Our passions transcended
What in seriousness repelled us

And she bid me close my eyes
And behold some dreadful magnificence

Running ice
Cold pulse

Memories of iceday icenight
She told me goodbye forever

A month later
A no-return-address letter came

"I've a snow owl
And it loves you it loves you"

Friend

Friends be kept
Friends be gained
And even friends lost be friends regained
He had no foes he made them all into *friends*
A friend will die for you
Acquaintances can never make friends
Some friends want to be everybody's friend
There are friends who take you away from friends
Friends believe in friendship with a vengeance!
Some friends always want to do you favors
Some always want to get NEAR you
You can't do this to me I'm your FRIEND
My friends said FDR
Let's be friends says the USSR
Old Scrooge knew a joy in a friendless Christmas
Leopold and Loeb planning in the night!
Et tu Brute
I have many friends yet sometimes I am nobody's friend
The majority of friends are male
Girls always prefer male friends
Friends know when you're troubled
It's what they crave for!
The bonds of friendship are not inseparable
Those who haven't any friends and want some are often creepy
Those who have friends and don't want them are doomed
Those who haven't any friends and don't want any are grand
Those who have friends and want them seem sadly human
Sometimes I scream Friends are bondage! A madness!
All a waste of INDIVIDUAL *time*—
Without friends life would be different not miserable
Does one need a friend in heaven—

Halloween

Children and many strangely things
wait their wings
watching yellow leaves and a red sun fall—
There goes Bunch Bunch haycocking
the Octob'rian argosy
he's a great bushel of apples
and now a black sky
now an orange sea—
Within Groot's twisted oaky gnarl
by a pumpkin's grinning glow
the wingmaker in chaste leprosy does sew
His owl suspects the broom
The mean cat as usual is scared out of its wits
and in a little dark corner
        trembles the entire room—

Stars

Central the hole of creation
Escape hatch from impending light
Uncreatures of space leap out
—Vivid fossils embedded in the night

Seed Journey

There they go
and where they stop
trees will grow

The nuts of amnesiac squirrels
more nuts will be
Bur takes freight on animal fur
And pollen the wind does carry

For some seeds
bread is the end of the journey

The Saving Quality

Bad nights of drunk
make bad days of sorry

Last night was stained with fear
I or the world was all wrong

Today in hard wind and rain
I stand on Putney's bridge
flinging Ritz crackers to the swans
ducks and gulls below
assuring myself:
      day or night
      you're all right

A Difference of Zoos

I went to the Hotel Broog;
and it was there I imagined myself singing *Ave Maria*
      to a bunch of hoary ligneous Brownies.
I believe in gnomes, in midges;
I believe to convert the bogeyman,
take Medusa to Kenneth's;
beg Zeus Polyphemus a new eye;
and I thanked all the men who ever lived,
thanked life the world
      for the chimera, the gargoyle,
      the sphinx, the griffin,
      Rumpelstiltskin—
I sang *Ave Maria*
      for the Heap, for Groot,
      for the mugwump, for Thoth,
      the centaur, Pan;
I summoned them all to my room in the Broog,
the werewolf, the vampire, Frankentstein
every monster imaginable
and sang and sang *Ave Maria—*
The room got to be unbearable!
I went to the zoo
and oh thank God the simple elephant.

Some Greek Writings

for Bill Barker & Miss Portman

IN A WAY
the Greeks today
don't like the Acropolis
because
it hovers over them
as though mockingly
as though imprisoning them
in a you-can't-do-better-than-me
      abyss

No matter whicheverway
they look
that mark of history
      is impossible to miss

WHEN PRESIDENT EISENHOWER
came to Athens
he got a helicopter
and flew over the Acropolis
and looked down at it
      like only Zeus could

I told that to a sharp Englishman
who replied:
He's fortunate he did not fly over it
      like Icarus

112

PHAESTOS IS A VILLAGE WITH 25 FAMILIES
and one taverna
There my friend and I sat
drinking with the tallest Greek in the world
And though he must have been close to sixty
his face and body seemed those of a strong young prince
We could not speak each other's language
but drink after drink we talked about everything

I learned by my little German
and my companion's little Greek
and the others their little French and English
"He shot twenty German officers"
"But he wouldn't shoot a soldier"
"He says they were young and good"
"Now that the war is over and no more officers
        he's unhappy"
"He's unhappy because the village has forgotten
        his heroics"
He sighed a sigh which seemed to say:
Those were the good old days
Having drunk so much I had to go to the toilet
and so did my friend and almost all the others
There was no toilet

Thus out into the pitch dark we staggered
behind the taverna we went
where
beneath the starriest sky I ever saw
we all did wondrously pee

Active Night

A tarsier bewrays the end of an epical rain
Burying beetles ponderously lug a dead rat
A moth, just a few seconds old, tumbles down fern
Bats are drinking flowers
The lonely tapir walks the river bottom
And up comes a manatee with a sea-anemone
       on its nose

A Race of Sound

Sounds are running a race the trek the climb the swim
       the pace
And voices are edging up to roars and close behind
       the closing of doors the thump of rabbits
And coming up in the stretch the howling of ghosts
The humming of birds and now voices are neck and neck
With the climb of vines and the trek of penguins
The swim of fish is third and moving in the inside thunder
       and bombs and in the back stretch the thud of coffins
       the fall of timber the sway of palms
Voices are leading are leading heaving and breathing
       speaking and singing fully in the clear but hold hold
From out of nowhere the wail of cats the chomp of carrots
A squeaky shoe challenges for the lead Oh what a race!
Here comes the drop of a pin the cawk of a parrot
The breaking of glass the scratch of an itch
The crowds are going wild! yelling and kicking and jumping
—so wild they win the race

Writ on the Steps of Puerto Rican Harlem

There's a truth limits man
A truth prevents his going any farther
The world is changing
The world *knows* it's changing
Heavy is the sorrow of the day
The old have the look of doom
The young mistake their fate in that look
That is truth
But it isn't *all* truth

Life has meaning
And I do not know the meaning
Even when I felt it were meaningless
I hoped and prayed and sought a meaning
It wasn't all frolic poesy
There were dues to pay
Summoning Death and God
I'd a wild dare to tackle Them
Death proved meaningless without Life
Yes the world is changing
But Death remains the same
It takes man away from Life
The only meaning he knows
And usually it is a sad business
This Death

I'd an innocence I'd a seriousness
I'd a humor save me from amateur philosophy
I am able to contradict my beliefs
I am able able
Because I want to know the meaning of everything

Yet sit I like a brokenness
Moaning: Oh what responsibility
I put on thee Gregory
Death and God
Hard hard it's hard

I learned life were no dream
I learned truth deceived
Man is not God
Life is a century
Death an instant

They

They, that unnamed "they,"
they've knocked me down
    but I got up
I always get up—
And I swear when I went down
    quite often I took the fall;
nothing moves a mountain but itself—
They, I've long ago named them me.

For—

What stinking beady wart
    like a ten ton toad
squats on life's sick nose
    puffing molten mega-pus
ever ready to hop upon the earth
    and splash all over us

The bomb's a decoy
I've seen the horror of narcotics
    eat the day
They were all sad
sad mainly because life was insufficient
They were sickly sad
And drugs were a filthy nurse

Danger

Because of me narcotics are—
Useless you enforcers of safety
scheming ways and hows to keep out of me;
there is no out, there is only in,
and you are all in danger—

Useless to deface the world with:
Beware, Do Not Trespass, Skullcrossbones,
E Pericoloso Sporgersi—
My property is sorrow!
No fence.
No warning there—

Second Night in N.Y.C. After 3 Years

I was happy I was bubbly drunk
The street was dark
I waved to a young policeman
He smiled
I went up to him and like a flood of gold
Told him all about my prison youth
About how noble and great the convicts were
And about how I just returned from Europe
Which wasn't half as enlightening as prison
And he listened attentively I told no lie
Everything was truth and humor
He laughed
He laughed
And it made me so happy I said:
"Absolve it all, kiss me!"
"No no no no!" he said
      and hurried away.

Writ on the Eve of My 32nd Birthday

a slow thoughtful spontaneous poem

I am 32 years old
and finally I look my age, if not more.
Is it a good face what's no more a boy's face?
It seems fatter. And my hair,
it's stopped being curly. Is my nose big?
The lips are the same.
And the eyes, ah the eyes get better all the time.
32 and no wife, no baby; no baby hurts,
        but there's lots of time.
I don't act silly any more.
And because of it I have to hear from so-called friends:
"You've changed. You used to be so crazy so great."
They are not comfortable with me when I'm serious.
Let them go to the Radio City Music Hall.
32; saw all of Europe, met millions of people;
        was great for some, terrible for others.
I remember my 31st year when I cried:
"To think I may have to go another 31 years!"
I don't feel that way this birthday.
I feel I want to be wise with white hair in a tall library
        in a deep chair by a fireplace.
Another year in which I stole nothing.
8 years now and haven't stole a thing!
I stopped stealing!
But I still lie at times,
and still am shameless yet ashamed when it comes
        to asking for money.
32 years old and four hard real funny sad bad wonderful
        books of poetry
—the world owes me a million dollars.

I think I had a pretty weird 32 years.
And it weren't up to me, none of it.
No choice of two roads; if there were,
    I don't doubt I'd have chosen both.
I like to think *chance* had it I play the bell.
The clue, perhaps, is in my unabashed declaration:
"I'm good example there's such a thing as called soul."
I love poetry because it makes me love
    and presents me life.
And of all the fires that die in me,
there's one burns like the sun;
it might not make day my personal life,
    my association with people,
    or my behavior toward society,
but it does tell me my soul has a shadow.

From **ELEGIAC FEELINGS AMERICAN**

Elegiac Feelings American

for the dear memory of John Kerouac

1

How inseparable you and the America you saw yet was
        never there to see; you and America, like the
        tree and the ground, are one the same; yet how
        like a palm tree in the state of Oregon . . . dead
        ere it blossomed, like a snow polar loping the
        Miami—
How so that which you were or hoped to be, and the
        America not, the America you saw yet could
        not see
So like yet unlike the ground from which you stemmed;
        you stood upon America like a rootless
        flat-bottomed tree; to the squirrel there was no
        divorcement in its hop of ground to its climb of
        tree . . . until it saw no acorn fall, then it knew
        there was no marriage between the two; how
        fruitless, how useless, the sad unnaturalness
        of nature; no wonder the dawn ceased being
        a joy . . . for what good the earth and sun when
        the tree in between is good for nothing . . .
        the inseparable trinity, once dissevered, becomes a
        cold fruitless meaningless thrice-marked
        deathlie in its awful amputation . . . O butcher
        the pork-chop is not the pig—The American
        alien in America is a bitter truncation; and even
        this elegy, dear Jack, shall have a butchered
        tree, a tree beaten to a pulp, upon which it'll be
        contained—no wonder no good news can be
        written on such bad news—

How alien the natural home, aye, aye, how dies the tree
          when the ground is foreign, cold, unfree—The
          winds know not to blow the seed of the
          Redwood where none before stood; no palm is
          blown to Oregon, how wise the wind—Wise
          too the senders of the prophet . . . knowing the
          fertility of the designated spot where suchmeant
          prophecy be announced and answerable—the
          sower of wheat does not sow in the fields of
          cane; for the sender of the voice did also send
          the ear. And were little Liechtenstein, and not
          America, the designation . . . surely then we'd
          the tongues of Liechtenstein—
Was not so much our finding America as it was America
          finding its voice in us; many spoke to America
          as though America by land-right was theirs by
          law-right legislatively acquired by materialistic
          coups of wealth and inheritance; like the citizen
          of society believes himself the owner of society,
          and what he makes of himself he makes of
          America and thus when he speaks of America
          he speaks of himself, and quite often such a he
          is duly elected to represent what he represents . . .
          an infernal ego of an America
Thus many a patriot speaks lovingly of himself when he
          speaks of America, and not to appreciate him is
          not to appreciate America, and vice-versa
The tongue of truth is the true tongue of America, and it
          could not be found in the *Daily Heralds* since
          the voice therein was a controlled voice,
          wickedly opinionated, and directed at gullible
No wonder we found ourselves rootless . . . for we've become
          the very roots themselves,—the lie can never
          take root and there grow under a truth of sun
          and therefrom bear the fruit of truth

Alas, Jack, seems I cannot requiem thee without
            requieming America, and that's one requiem
            I shall not presume, for as long as I live there'll
            be no requiems for me
For though the tree dies the tree is born anew, only until
            the tree dies forever and never a tree born
            anew . . . shall the ground die too
Yours the eyes that saw, the heart that felt, the voice that
            sang and cried; and as long as America shall
            live, though ye old Kerouac body hath died,
            yet shall you live . . . for indeed ours was a time
            of prophecy without death as a consequence . . .
            for indeed after us came the time of assassins,
            and who'll doubt thy last words "After me . . .
            the deluge"
Ah, but were it a matter of seasons I'd not doubt the return
            of the tree, for what good the ground upon
            which we stand itself unable to stand—aye the
            tree will in seasonal time fall, for it be nature's
            wont, that's why the ground, the down, the slow
            yet sure decomposition, until the very tree
            becomes the very ground where once it stood;
            yet falls the ground . . . ah, then what?
            unanswerable this be unto nature, for there is
            no ground whereon to fall and land, no down,
            no up even, directionless, and into what, if what,
            composition goeth its decomposition?
We came to announce the human spirit in the name of
            beauty and truth; and now this spirit cries out in
            nature's sake the horrendous imbalance of all
            things natural . . . elusive nature caught! like a
            bird in hand, harnessed and engineered in the
            unevolutional ways of experiment and technique

Yes though the tree has taken root in the ground the ground
is upturned and in this forced vomitage is spewn
the dire miasma of fossilific trees of death the
million-yeared pitch and grease of a dinosauric
age dead and gone how all brought to surface
again and made to roam the sky we breathe in
stampedes of pollution
What hope for the America so embodied in thee, O friend,
when the very same alcohol that disembodied
your brother redman of his America,
disembodied ye—A plot to grab their land, we
know—yet what plot to grab the ungrabbable
land of one's spirit? Thy visionary America were
impossible to unvision—for when the shades of
the windows of the spirit are brought down, that
which was seen yet remains . . . the eyes of the
spirit yet see
Aye the America so embodied in thee, so definitely rooted
therefrom, is the living embodiment of all
humanity, young and free
And though the great redemptive tree blooms, not yet full,
not yet entirely sure, there be the darksters, sad
and old, would like to have it fall; they hack
and chop and saw away . . . that nothing full
and young and free for sure be left to stand at
all
Verily were such trees as youth be . . . were such be made
to fall, and never rise to fall again, then shall
the ground fall, and the deluge come and wash
it asunder, wholly all and forever, like a wind
out of nowhere into nowhere

2

"How so like Clark Gable hands your hands. . ." (Mexico
conversation 1956)—Hands so strong and
Mexican sunned, busy about America, hands I
knew would make it, would hold guard and
caring

You were always talking about America, and America
            was always history to me, General Wolfe lying
            on the ground dying in his bright redcoat
            smittered by a bluecoat hanging in the classroom
            wall next to the father of our country whose
            heart area was painted in cloud . . . yes, ours
            was an American history, a history with a
            future, for sure;
How a Whitman we were always wanting, a hoping, an
            America, that America ever an America to be,
            never an America to sing about or to, but ever
            an America to sing hopefully for
All we had was past America, and ourselves, the now
            America, and O how we regarded that past!
            And O the big lie of that school classroom! The
            Revolutionary War . . . all we got was
            Washington, Revere, Henry, Hamilton, Jefferson,
            and Franklin . . . never Nat Bacon, Sam Adams,
            Paine . . . and what of liberty? was not to gain
            liberty that war, liberty they had, they were the
            freest peoples of their time; was not to *lose* that
            liberty was why they went to arms—yet, and
            yet, the season that blossomed us upon the scene
            was hardly free; be there liberty today? not to
            hear the redman, the blackman, the youngman
            tell—
And in the beginning when liberty was all one could hear;
            wasn't much of it for the poor witches of Salem;
            and that great lauder of liberty, Franklin, paid
            100 dollar bounty for each scalp of the wild
            children of natural free; Pitt Jr. obtained most of
            the city of brotherly love by so outrageous a
            deception as stymied the trusting heart of his
            red brother with tortuous mistrust; and how
            ignorant of liberty the wise Jefferson owning the
            black losers of liberty; for the declarers of
            independence to declare it only for part of the
            whole was to declare civil war

Justice is all any man of liberty need hope for; and justice
            was a most important foundling thing; a diadem
            for American life upon which the twinship of
            private property and God could be established;
How suffered the poor native American the enforced
            establishing of those two pillars of liberty!
From justice stems a variable God, from God stems a
            dictated justice
"The ways of the Lord lead to liberty" sayeth St. Paul . . .
            yet a man need liberty, not God, to be able to
            follow the ways of God
The justness of individual land right is not justifiable to
            those to whom the land by right of first claim
            collectively belonged;
He who sells mankind's land to a single man sells the
            Brooklyn Bridge
The second greatest cause of human death . . . is the
            acquiring of property
No American life is worth an acre of America . . . if No
            Trespassing and guarding mastiffs can't tell you
            shotguns will
So, sweet seeker, just what America sought you anyway?
            Know that today there are millions of Americans
            seeking America . . . know that even with all
            those eye-expanding chemicals—only more of
            what is not there do they see
Some find America in songs of clumping stone, some in
            fogs of revolution
All find it in their hearts . . . and O how it tightens the heart
Not so much their being imprisoned in an old and
            unbearable America . . . more the America
            imprisoned in them—so wracks and darkens the
            spirit
An America unseen, dreamed, tremors uncertain, bums the
            heart, sends bad vibes forth cosmic and
            otherwise
You could see the contempt in their young-sad eyes . . . and
            meantime the jails are becoming barber shops,
            and the army has always been

Yet unable they are to shave the hurricane from their eyes
Look unto Moses, no prophet ever reached the dreamed of
      lands . . . ah but your eyes are dead . . . nor the
      America beyond your last dreamed hill hovers
      real

3

How alike our hearts and time and dying, how our America
      out there and in our hearts insatiable yet
      overflowing hallelujahs of poesy and hope
How we knew to feel each dawn, to ooh and aah each
      golden sorrow and helplessness coast to coast
      in our search for whatever joy steadfast never
      there nowever grey
Yea the America the America unstained and never
      revolutioned for liberty ever in us free, the
      America in us—unboundaried and unhistoried,
      we the America, we the fathers of that America,
      the America you Johnnyappleseeded, the
      America I heralded, an America not there, an
      America soon to be

The prophet affects the state, and the state affects the
      prophet—What happened to you, O friend,
      happened to America, and we know what
      happened to America—the stain . . . the stains,
O and yet when it's asked of you "What happened to him?"
      I say "What happened to America has happened
      him—the two were inseparable" Like the wind
      to the sky is the voice to the word. . . .
And now that voice is gone, and now the word is bone, and
      the America is going, the planet boned
A man can have everything he desires in his home yet have
      nothing outside the door—for a feeling man, a
      poet man, such an outside serves only to make
      home a place in which to hang oneself

And us ones, sweet friend, we've always brought America
    home with us—and never like dirty laundry, even
    with all the stains
And through the front door, lovingly cushioned in our
    hearts; where we sat down and told it our
    dreams of beauty
    hopeful that it would leave our homes beautiful
And what has happened to our dream of beauteous
    America, Jack?
Did it look beautiful to you, did it sound so too, in its cold
    electric blue, that America that spewed and
    stenched your home, your good brain, that
    unreal fake America, that caricature of America,
    that plugged in a wall America . . . a gallon of
    desperate whiskey a day it took ye to look that
    America in its disembodied eye
And it saw you not, it never saw you, for what you saw was
    not there, what you saw was Laugh-in, and all
    America was in laughing, that America brought
    you in, brought America in, all that out there
    brought in, all that nowhere nothing in, no
    wonder you were lonesome, died empty and
    sad and lonely, you the real face and voice . . .
    caught before the fake face and voice—and it
    became real and you fake,
O the awful fragility of things

"What happened to him?" "What happened to you?" Death
    happened him; a gypped life happened; a God
    gone sick happened; a dream nightmared; a
    youth armied; an army massacred; the father
    wants to eat the son, the son feeds his stone,
    but the father no get stoned
And you, Jack, poor Jack, watched your father die, your
    America die, your God die, your body die, die
    die die; and today fathers are watching their
    sons die, and their sons are watching babies die,
    why? Why? How we both asked WHY?
O the sad sad awfulness of it all

You but a mere decade of a Kerouac, but what a lifetime in
    that dix Kerouac!
Nothing happened you that did not happen; nothing went
    unfulfilled, you circ'd the circle full, and what's
    happening to America is no longer happening
    to you, for what happens to the consciousness
    of the land happens to the voice of that
    consciousness and the voice has died yet the
    land remains to forget what it has heard and the
    word leaves no bone
And both word and land of flesh and earth suffer the same
    sick the same death . . . and dies the voice
    before the flesh, and the wind blows a dead
    silence over the dying earth, and the earth will
    leave its bone, and nothing of wind will roll the
    moan, but silence, silence, nor e'en that will
    God's ear hear

Aye, what happened to you, dear friend, compassionate
    friend, is what is happening to everyone and
    thing of planet the clamorous sadly desperate
    planet now one voice less . . . expendable as the
    wind . . . gone, and who'll now blow away the
    awful miasma of sick, sick and dying
    earthflesh-soul America

When you went on the road looking for America you found
    only what you put there and a man seeking gold
    finds the only America there is to find; and his
    investment and a poet's investment . . . the same
    when comes the crash, and it's crashing, yet
    the windows are tight, are not for jumping; from
    hell none e'er fell

4

In Hell angels sing too
And they sang to behold anew
Those who followed the first Christ-bearer
left hell and beheld a world new
yet with guns and Bibles came they
and soon their new settlement became old
and once again hell held quay
The ArcAngel Raphael was I to you
And I put the Cross of the Lord of Angels
upon you . . . there
on the eve of a new world to explore
And you were flashed upon the old and darkling day
a Beat Christ-boy . . . bearing the gentle roundness of things
insisting the soul was round not square
And soon . . . behind thee
there came a-following
the children of flowers

North Beach, San Francisco, 1969

Spontaneous Requiem for the American Indian

Wakonda! Talako! deathonic turkey gobbling in the soft-
    footpatch night!
Blue-tipped yellow-tipped red-tipped feathers of whort dye
    fluffing in fire mad dance whaa whaa dead men red
    men feathers-in-their-head-men night!
Deerskin rage of flesh on the bone on the hot tobacco
    ground!
Muskhogean requiems america southeastern, O death of
    Creeks, Choctaws,
The youthful tearful Brave, in his dying hand trout, well-
    caught proud trout,
Softest of feet, fleet, o america dirge, o america norwegians
    swedes of quid and murder and boots and slaughter
    and God and rot-letters,
O pinto brays! O deatheme sled mourning the dying chief!
Berries, spruce, whortle, cranky corn, bitter wheat; o scarcity
    of men!
High-throttled squawlark, sister warrior, teepee maid, scar
    lover, crash down thy muskrat no longer thy flesh
    hand and rage and writhe and pound thy Indianic
    earth with last pang of love of love,
O america, o requiems—

Ghost-herds of uneaten left to rot animals thundering across
    the plains
Chasing the ghost of England across the plains forever ever,
    pompous Kiwago raging in the still Dakotas, o amer-
    ica—
America o mineral scant america o mineralize america o
    conferva of that once

great lovely Muskhogean pool, o oil-suck america despite,
 oil from forgetive days, hare to arrow, muskellunge to
 spear, fleet-footed know ye speed-well the tribes
 thence outraced the earth to eat to love to die,
o requiems, Hathor off-far bespeaks Wakonda,
heraldic henequen tubas whittled in coyote tune to mourn
 the death of the going sun the going sled of each
 dying, sad and dying, shake of man, the tremble of
 men, of each dying chief slow and red and leather
 fur hot—
Shake slow the rattler, the hawk-teeth, the bettle-bells,
 shake slow dirge, o dirge, shake slow the winds of
 winds, o feathers withered and blown,
Dirge the final pinto-led sled, the confused hurt sad king of
 Montanas,
Strike dumb the French fur trappers in their riverboat brool
 mockery, no chant of death in such a wealth of musk-
 rat and beaver, shun them,
O slam squaw hysteria down on america, the covered wagon
 america, the arrow flamed wagons of conquest, the
 death stand of quakers and white-hooded hags and
 proud new men, young and dead,
O Geronimo! hard nickel faced Washington Boliva of a
 dying city that never was, that monster-died, that
 demons gathered to steal and did,
O Sitting Bull! pruneman Jefferson Lenin Lincoln reddead-
 man, force thy spirit to wings, cloud the earth to air,
 o the condor the vulture the hawk fat days are gone,
 and you are gone, o america, o requiems,
Dry valleys, deathhead stones, high Arizonas, red sun earth,
 the sled,
The weeping bray, the ponymarenight, the slow chief of
 death, wrinkled and sad and manless, vistaless, smoke-
 less, proud sad dying—
Toward the coyote reach of peak and moon, howl of hey-
 day, laugh proud of men and men, Blackfoot, Mo-
 hawk, Algonquin, Seneca, all men, o american, peaked
 there then bow

Thy white-haired straw head and, pinto imitated, die with
the rising moon, hotnight, lost, empty, unseen, music-
less, mindless; no wind—
In the grim dread light of the Happy Hunting Ground
A century of chiefs argue their many scalps, whacking the
yellow strands of a child against the coaly misty
harsh of tent;
It falls apart in a scatter of strewn, away, gone, no more,
back free out of the quay into the bladder seep of
the bald dead seeking the hairless rawhead child of
whiteman's grave;
O there is more an exact sorrow in this Indianical eternity,
Sure o america woof and haw and caw and wooooo whirl
awhirl here o weep!
Indianhill woe! never was the scalp of men the prime knife
in the heart of a savagengence era, Clevelandestroyer
of manland, o requiems,
O thundercloud, thunderbird, rain-in-the-face, hark in the
gloom, death,
And blankets and corn, and peaceful footings of man in
quest of Kiwago, america, Kiwago, america, corn
america, earthly song of a sad boy's redfleshed song
in the night before the peered head intrusive head of
laughing thunderbolt Zeus, o the prank, o the death,
o the night,
Requiem, america, sing a dirge that might stalk the white
wheat black in praise of Indianever again to be, gone,
gone, desolate, and gone;
Hear the plains, the great divide, hear the wind of this night
Oklahoma race to weep first in the dirge of mountains
and streams and trees and birds and day and night
and the bright yet lost apparitional sled,
The bowed head of an Indian is enough to bow the horse's
head and both in unison die and die and die and
never again die for once the night eats up the dying
it eats up the pain and there is no Indian pain no
pregnant squaw no wild-footed great-eyed boy no
jolly stern fat white-furred chief of tobacco damp
and sweet, o america america—

Each year Kiwago must watch its calves thin out; must
        watch with all its natural killers dead, the new
        marksmen of machines and bullets and trained stud-
        ied eyes aim and fire and kill the oldest bull, the king,
        the Kiwago of the reminiscent plain—
Each year Wakonda must watch the motionless desert, the
        dry tearless childless desert, the smokeless desert, the
        Indianlessadly desert—
Each year Talako must watch the bird go arrowless in his
        peace of sky in his freedom of the mouth of old
        america, raw wild calm america,
O america, o requiem, o tumbleweed, o Western Sky, each
        year is another year the soft football doesn't fall, the
        thin strong arm of spear never raised, the wise coun-
        cil of gathered kings no longer warm with life and
        fur and damp and heat and hotcorn and dry jerky
        meat, each year no squaw titters her moony lover of
        hard love and necessary need of man and wife and
        child child, each year no child, no mien of life, good
        life, no, no, america, but the dead stones, the dry
        trees, the dusty going winded earth—requiem.

Pilgrim blunderbuss, buckles, high hat, Dutch, English, pat-
ent leather shoes, Bible, pray, snow, careful, careful, o but
feast, turkey, corn, pumpkin, sweet confused happy hosty
guests, Iroquois, Mohawk, Oneida, Onondaga, Thanksgiving!
O joy! o angels! o peace! o land! land land land,
        o death,
O fire and arrow and buckshot and whisky and rum and
        death and land,
O witches and taverns and quakers and Salem and New
        Amsterdam and corn,
And night, softfeet, death, massacre, massacre, o america,
        o requiem—
Log-cabins, forts, outposts, trading-posts, in the distance,
        clouds,

Dust, hordes, tribes, death, death, blonde girls to die, gowns
     of ladies to burn, men of redcoats and bluecoats to
     die, boys to drum and fife and curse and cry and die,
     horses . . . to die, babies . . . to die;

Yeeeeeeeeeeeeeeeooooooooooo! Harrrrrrrrrrrrrraaaaaaaaaa!
EEEEEEEEeeeeeee EEEEEEaaaaaaaaaaaaah!
To die to die to die to die to die . . . america, requiem.
Corn, jerky, whortly, the Seneca in a deacon's suit, gawky,
     awkward, drunk,
Tired, slouched—the gowns and bright boots pass, the quick
take-your-partner-swing-to-the-left-swing-to-the-right hums
all is over, done, the Seneca sleeps, no sled, no pinto, no end,
but sleep, and a new era, a new day, a new light and the
corn grows plenty, and the night is forever, and the day;

The jetliner streams down upon Texas,
            Requiem.

Motorcyclist Blackfoot his studded belt at night wilder than
bright hawkeyes sits on his fat bike black smelly brusqued
assy about to goggleeye himself down golden ventures whiz-
zing faster than his ancestral steed past smokestacks banner-
shacks O the timid shade of Kiwago now! the mad roar
exhaustpipe Indian like a fleeing oven clanking weeeeee
weeeeeee no feathers in his oily helmet O he's a fast engine
of steam zooming unlaurelled by but he's stupid he sits in
Horn & Hardart's his New York visit and he's happy with
his short girls with pink faces and bright hair talking about
his big fat bike and their big fat bike, O he's an angel there
though sinister sinister in shape of Steel Discipline smoking
a cigarette in a fishy corner in the night, waiting, america,
waiting the end, the last Indian, mad Indian of no fish or
foot or proud forest haunt, mad on his knees ponytailing &
rabbitfooting his motorcycle, his the final requiem the final
america READY THE FUNERAL STOMP goodluck charms
on, tires aired, spikes greased, morose goggles on, motor gas
brakes checked! 1958 Indians, heaps of leather—ZOOM
down the wide amber speedway of Death, Little Richard,
tuba mirum, the vast black jacket brays in the full forced fell.

Lines Written Nov. 22, 23–1963
—in Discord—

So what's it like being an American Assassin this silly
    uncertain day?

Not I with chiromancerian eyes
  Do I raise my right hand that Popes halt
  Talmudians relent?
Like a table of fishy Chinamen
  I laugh my purpose into dopey disguise
Who'll see this
  or that
  or where-they're-at
bereft of such eyes?

      The Good   The Bad
      I seek the Good
      But *I Am* Good!
      Thus the bad, O damn, O thank God, I'm sure to find.

Heed me all you creepy goopy assassins!
    I am a million jinns! I build ins and outs and ins!
I'm all them gremlins! dropping wrenches
    in BOAC's BOEINGS
    . . . sticking pins in zeppelins!
O I am a zillion million stars twinkling in the all crazy fars!
I am innumerable illuminable sins!
    I am indoomable ingloomable
And the uncreation of the world is the work of every
    humanable human imaginable!
    —all are assassins!
And I swear to you are Indians less cruel no I swear to you
    hashish has never been your gruel
    you drunken inexorbitant square killer non-hashadins!

One poke of red-eyed hash would make all of you hail it
        iatrical not homicidal not rifle not Presidental
Aye you are punk killers not assassins!
Ah, the Disney dinosaur's light laughter & a little blonde
        girl's tears
What sad what sick what damned juxtaposition!
        monster and child, punk and President
        society and poet, bullets and flesh
Bullets the size of Coney Island Fishing worms
        can obliterate blix pow-out the whole shebang
No man's the whole bit
But that young President was more than a little bit
The captain should go down when his ship goes down
But when the captain dies . . . the ship sails on—
O failure Christ

Come you illiterate creepy dumbbells harken the cry of
        the *true* Assassin
        I damn! I hail!
I summon the Blessed Lord of the Ice Cold Nanook Country
        and eat raw seal meat with Him!
I curse the earth in Space and in Time!
I pee upon the Evolution of the Rocks!
I weep upon the first living things!
Bang my fists on the unknown age of the world!
I vomit up Natural Selection and the Change of the Species!
I laugh like a sick dinosaur o'er
        the invasion of the dry lands by Life!
I smirk at the butterfly like a pimply-faced stumble-bum!
By the wings I yank by the wings the wings the lovely wings
By the throat I smote the Age of the Reptile!
So too the Age of the Mammal!
So too O very much so the Ancestry of Man!
Man descended from a walking ape!
I awake the lazy greasy Neanderthal and spit in his big sad
        stupid eye!
I pummel my Colt .38 into the iron skin of the Palaeolithic
        muralist!
I look contemptuously down upon the screwed-up Neolithic
        creep!

I beckon the coming of those early bastards much like
      ourselves today and blow a sadistic breath of death
      in their hoary faces!

O orange owls! O ambitious green!
I sneak upon the beginning of earth's cultivation
      and sow poisoned polly-seeds
      ahead of the prehistoric farmer's burning reap
I am there at the flooding of the Mediterranean Valley
      and watch the thousand life drown and die!
I enter the earliest thought, the most primitive philosophy,
      and drive mad dreams and sick fears into the Old
      Man, the Priest, the Vestal
I turn the stars and seasons into giant hideous creatures!
I inject the word cancer the word kill the word hate into
      the Aryan tongue
      the Semitic tongue
      the Hamitic Ural-Altaic and Chink tongues!
I am there watching the earliest nomads stop to build Ur,
      Sumer
I shall strike a flashlight into the Sumerians' eyes and
      mystify them nuts!
I have poisoned Sargon! Stabbed Hammurabi!
      Like the Pest I wiped out the Assyrians!
      the Chaldeans!
I grabbed the history of ancient Egypt and India and China
      and infested it with the big lie of Bel-Marduk
      and God-Kings
      and ordered Shi Hwang-ti, like a dowser a goat,
      to destroy all records!
I have made goats of every King every Pope every puny
      clubbed-foot Elect
      in every chapter of that history I puke up like bile
      . . . like bile

Now the Rains of Darkness begin
The entire stellified crop   out!
Sags the wick like a limp giraffe neck   like a sick nose

And lo! on the back of a wet firefly
    comes Hi-Fi
    yet mournful   yet I am the one to suffer
    whose thousand years attempt at being
        the Great Assassinator
    has failed to dump even Methuselah

    O brown fortune! I shake your devils!
So small am I to the proportion of so small a tree
And a sun so small in that sunny sea called Eternity
Insignificant sun! Lamp of lard! Bright ant faked God!
    Conjurer of string beans!
O so small am I   and smaller the things I eat and believe
    O tiny Adam O shrimp Eve
So it is   So it shall come to be
The gap caused by my magnified midgetry shall become
    someday like all great China
    the China basin for the new China sea!
And so Kennedy   and so America
    and so A and so B and so C
With a full arrow and ½ bow   I'll lay em low

    O Lord of Ducks! O Fame of Death!
    When a captain dies
    The ship doesn't sink
    And though the crew weeps the loss
    The stars in the skies
    are still boss.

The American Way

1

I am a great American
I am almost nationalistic about it!
I love America like a madness!
But I am afraid to return to America
I'm even afraid to go into the American Express—

2

They are frankensteining Christ in America
    in their Sunday campaigns
They are putting the fear of Christ in America
    under their tents in their Sunday campaigns
They are driving old ladies mad with Christ in America
They are televising the gift of healing and the fear of hell
    in America under their tents in their Sunday
    campaigns
They are leaving their tents and are bringing their Christ
    to the stadiums of America in their Sunday
    campaigns
They are asking for a full house an all get out
    for their Christ in the stadiums of America
They are getting them in their Sunday and Saturday
    campaigns
They are asking them to come forward and fall on their
    knees
       because they are all guilty and they are coming
       forward
       in guilt and are falling on their knees weeping their
       guilt
       begging to be saved O Lord O Lord in their Monday
    Tuesday Wednesday Thursday Friday Saturday
    and Sunday campaigns

3

It is a time in which no man is extremely wondrous
It is a time in which rock stupidity
          outsteps the 5th Column as the sole enemy in America
It is a time in which ignorance is a good Ameri-cun
          ignorance is excused only where it is so
          it is not so in America
Man is not guilty   Christ is not to be feared
I am telling you the American Way is a hideous monster
          eating Christ   making Him into Oreos and Dr. Pepper
          the sacrament of its foul mouth
I am telling you the devil is impersonating Christ in America
America's educators & preachers are the mental-dictators
          of false intelligence   they will not allow America
          to be smart
          they will only allow death to make America smart
Educators & communicators are the lackeys of the
          American Way
They enslave the minds of the young
          and the young are willing slaves (but not for long)
          because who is to doubt the American Way
          is not the way?
The duty of these educators is no different
          than the duty of a factory foreman
Replica production   make all the young think alike
          dress alike   believe alike   do alike
Togetherness   this is the American Way
The few great educators in America are weak & helpless
They abide   and so uphold the American Way
Wars have seen such men   they who despised things about
          them
          but did nothing   and they are the most dangerous
Dangerous because their intelligence is not denied
          and so give faith to the young
          who rightfully believe in their intelligence
Smoke this cigarette doctors smoke this cigarette
          and doctors know

Educators know   but they dare not speak their know
The victory that is man is made sad in this fix
Youth can only know the victory of being born
        all else is stemmed   until death be the final victory
        and a merciful one at that
If America falls it will be the blame of its educators
        preachers   communicators   alike
America today is America's greatest threat
We are old when we are young
America is always new   the world is always new
The meaning of the world is birth not death
Growth gone in the wrong direction
The true direction grows ever young
In this direction what grows grows old
A strange mistake   a strange and sad mistake
        for it has grown into an old thing
        while all else around it is new
Rockets will not make it any younger—
And what made America decide to grow?
I do not know   I can only hold it to the strangeness in man
And America has grown into the American Way—
To be young is to be ever purposeful   limitless
To grow is to know limit   purposelessness
Each age is a new age
How outrageous it is that something old and sad
        from the pre-age incorporates each new age—
Do I say the Declaration of Independence is old?
Yes   I say what was good for 1789 is not good for 1960
It was right and new to say all men were created equal
        because it was a light then
But today it is tragic to say it
        today it should be fact—
Man has been on earth a long time
One would think with his mania for growth
        he would, by now, have outgrown such things as
        constitutions manifestos codes commandments
        that he could well live in the world without them
        and know instinctively how to live and be
        —for what is being but the facility to love?

Was not that the true goal of growth, love?
Was not that Christ?
But man is strange and grows where he will
     and chalks it all up to Fate   whatever be—
America rings with such strangeness
It has grown into something strange and
     the American is good example of this mad growth
The boy man   big baby meat
     as though the womb were turned backwards
     giving birth to an old man
The victory that is man does not allow man
     to top off his empirical achievement with death
The Aztecs did it by yanking out young hearts
     at the height of their power
The Americans are doing it by feeding their young to the
     Way
For it was not the Spaniard who killed the Aztec
     but the Aztec who killed the Aztec
Rome is proof   Greece is proof   all history is proof
Victory does not allow degeneracy
It will not be the Communists will kill America
     no   but America itself—
The American Way   that sad mad process
     is not run by any one man or organization
It is a monster born of itself   existing of its self
The men who are employed by this monster
     are employed unknowingly
They reside in the higher echelons of intelligence
They are the educators the psychiatrists the ministers
     the writers the politicians the communicators
     the rich the entertainment world
And some follow and sing the Way because they sincerely
     believe it to be good
And some believe it holy and become minutemen in it
Some are in it simply to be in
And most are in it for gold
They do not see the Way as monster
They see it as the "Good Life"
What is the Way?

The Way was born out of the American Dream
        a nightmare—
The state of Americans today compared to the Americans
        of the 18th century proves the nightmare—
Not Franklin not Jefferson who speaks for America today
        but strange red-necked men of industry
        and the goofs of show business
Bizarre! Frightening! The Mickey Mouse sits on the throne
        and Hollywood has a vast supply—
Could grammar school youth seriously look upon
        a picture of George Washington and "Herman Borst"
        the famous night club comedian together at Valley
        Forge?
Old old and decadent   gone the dignity
        the American sun seems headed for the grave
O that youth might raise it anew!
The future depends solely on the young
The future is the property of the young
What the young know the future will know
What they are and do the future will be and do
What has been done must not be done again
Will the American Way allow this?
No.
I see in every American Express
        and in every army center in Europe
        I see the same face   the same sound of voice
        the same clothes   the same walk
I see mothers & fathers
        no difference among them
Replicas
They not only speak and walk and think alike
        they have the same face!
What did this monstrous thing?
What regiments a people so?
How strange is nature's play on America
Surely were Lincoln alive today
        he could never be voted President   not with his
        looks—

Indeed Americans are babies all in the embrace
       of Mama Way
Did not Ike, when he visited the American Embassy in
       Paris a year ago, say to the staff—"Everything is fine,
       just drink Coca Cola, and everything will be all right."
       This is true, and is on record
Did not American advertising call for TOGETHERNESS?
       not orgiasticly like today's call
       nor as means to stem violence
       This is true, and is on record.
Are not the army centers in Europe ghettos?
       They are, and O how sad   how lost!
The PX newsstands are filled with comic books
The army movies are always Doris Day
What makes a people huddle so?
Why can't they be universal?
Who has smalled them so?
This is serious! I do not mock or hate this
       I can only sense some mad vast conspiracy!
Helplessness is all it is!
They are caught   caught in the Way—
And those who seek to get out of the Way
       can not
The Beats are good example of this
They forsake the Way's habits
       and acquire for themselves their own habits
And they become as distinct and regimented and lost
       as the main flow
       because the Way has many outlets
       like a snake of many tentacles—
There is no getting out of the Way
The only way out is the death of the Way
And what will kill the Way but a new consciousness
Something great and new and wonderful must happen
       to free man from this beast
It is a beast we can not see or even understand
For it be the condition of our minds
God how close to science fiction it all seems!

As if some power from another planet
        incorporated itself in the minds of us all
It could well be!
For as I live I swear America does not seem like America
        to me

Americans are a great people
I ask for some great and wondrous event
        that will free them from the Way
        and make them a glorious purposeful people once
        again
I do not know if that event is due   deserved
        or even possible
I can only hold that man is the victory of life
And I hold firm to American man

I see standing on the skin of the Way
        America   to be as proud and victorious as St.
        Michael on the neck of the fallen Lucifer—

1961

Of One Month's Reading of English Newspapers

Ah, pierced is October; the tocsin tolls
And autumnographers wage their agriculture—
The temerity of a man sobs in a brush:
O God What Have I Done!
Pants down to ankles, bended knees,
Stunned head in hands—Sprawled beneath him
A baby virgina: a throated lambmess—bringing flies.
Girls of one to ten
Beware of Englishmen
All streets are lurk of them
Mary Dare? Art thou Mary Dare?
White Chapel Street is fog again
And girls are getting lost
—Is it Burke? Is it Hare?
The kind man behind the kind man
Is the kind of man who could and can
—Noon, slow, brool, a flowerian dress
Breezing over a flowerian face,
Sticky sex, sticky death, sticky sticky
Gold-eyed Regni in wolfic periscope
Loaming Surrey, Sussex,
Art thou Evans? Christie?
Girls of one to ten
Beware beware Englishmen
Dead month—corrupted October, dowsed octagon
Down to all conspired fossilry;
Mr. Jones stirs his homemade mead,
The girl scouts are near
The girl scouts are near—

America Politica Historia, in Spontaneity

O this political air so heavy with the bells
and motors of a slow night, and no place to rest
but rain to walk—How it rings the Washington streets!
The umbrella'd congressmen; the rapping tires
of big black cars, the shoulders of lobbyists
caught under canopies and in doorways,
and it rains, it will not let up,
and meanwhile lame futurists weep into Spengler's
prophecy, will the world be over before the races blend
        color?
All color must be one or let the world be done—
There'll be a chance, we'll all be orange!
I don't want to be orange!
Nothing about God's color to complain;
and there is a beauty in yellow, the old Lama
in his robe the color of Cathay;
in black a strong & vital beauty,
Thelonious Monk in his robe of Norman charcoal—
And if Western Civilization comes to an end
(though I doubt it, for the prophet has not
executed his prophecy) surely the Eastern child
will sit by a window, and wonder
the old statues, the ornamented doors;
the decorated banquet of the West—
Inflamed by futurists I too weep in rain at night
at the midnight of Western Civilization;
Dante's step into Hell will never be forgotten by Hell;
the Gods' adoption of Homer will never be forgotten by the
        Gods;
the books of France are on God's bookshelf;
no civil war will take place on the fields of God;
and I don't doubt the egg of the East its glory—

Yet it rains and the motors go
and continued when I slept by that wall in Washington
which separated the motors in the death-parlor
where Joe McCarthy lay, lean and stilled,
ten blocks from the Capitol—
I could never understand Uncle Sam
his red & white striped pants his funny whiskers his starry
        hat:
how surreal Yankee Doodle Dandy, goof!
American history has a way of making you feel
George Washington is still around, that is
when I think of Washington I do not think of Death—
Of all Presidents I have been under
Hoover is the most unreal
and FDR is the most President-looking
and Truman the most Jewish-looking
and Eisenhower the miscast of Time into Space—
Hoover is another America, Mr. 1930
and what must he be thinking now?
FDR was my youth, and how strange to still see
his wife around.
Truman is still in Presidential time.
I saw Eisenhower helicopter over Athens
and he looked at the Acropolis like only Zeus could.
OF THE PEOPLE is fortunate and select.
FOR THE PEOPLE has never happened in America or
        elsewhere.
BY THE PEOPLE is the sadness of America.
I am not politic.
I am not patriotic.
I am nationalistic!
I boast well the beauty of America to all the people in
        Europe.
In me they do not see their vision of America.
O whenever I pass an American Embassy I don't know what
        to feel!
Sometimes I want to rush in and scream: "I'm American!"
but instead go a few paces down to the American Bar
get drunk and cry: "I'm no American!"

The men of politics I love are but youth's fantasy:
The fine profile of Washington on coins stamps & tobacco
    wraps
The handsomeness and death-in-the-snow of Hamilton.
The eyeglasses shoe-buckles kites & keys of Ben Franklin.
The sweet melancholy of Lincoln.
The way I see Christ, as something romantic & unreal, is the
    way I see them.
An American is unique among peoples.
He looks and acts like a boyman.
He never looks cruel in uniform.
He is rednecked portly rich and jolly.
White-haired serious Harvard, kind and wry.
A convention man a family man a rotary man & practical
    joker.
He is moonfaced cunning well-meaning & righteously mean.
He is Madison Avenue, handsome, in-the-know, and
    superstitious.
He is odd, happy, quicker than light, shameless, and heroic
Great yawn of youth!
The young don't seem *interested* in politics anymore.
Politics has lost its romance!
The "bloody kitchen" has drowned!
And all that is left are those granite
façades of Pentagon, Justice, and Department—
Politicians do not know youth!
They depend on the old
and the old depend on them
and lo! this has given youth a chance
to think of heaven in their independence.
No need to give them liberty or freedom
where they're at—
When Stevenson in 1956 came to San Francisco
he campaigned in what he thought was an Italian section!
He spoke of Italy and Joe DiMaggio and spaghetti,
but all who were there, all for him,
were young beatniks! and when his car drove off
Ginsberg & I ran up to him and yelled:

"When are you going to free the poets from their attics!"
Great yawn of youth!
Mad beautiful oldyoung America has no candidate
the craziest wildest greatest country of them all!
and not one candidate—
Nixon arrives ever so temporal, self-made,
frontways sideways and backways,
could he be America's *against?* Detour to vehicle?
Mast to wind? Shore to sea? Death to life?
The last President?

God Is a Masturbator

Folks, sex has never been
more than a blend
of bodies doing for one
another
that which pleases
them and evolution
to do
either in desire
or in desperation
or in necessity
It serves no purpose
other than love
and life's purpose
Sexualists
are a product of sex
We are made by sex
Sex made the Salvation Army
We are sex
There is nothing dark
about this magic
And those pangs of lust
which make you sick
Those unthinkable dreams
which fill you with doubt
—as long as wild joys emit
from an enthusiastic spirit
eat the dust! *shout!*
Thank God one's thoughts
excite as much as flesh
Thank God there's a place
in all this he and she
and he and he
and she and she
for a me and me—

Ode to Old England & Its Language

To express what's seen, what's heard, imagined,
dreamed,
to hear, to read, to write, to speak—curse, console,
weep, laugh, O hybrid responsible irresponsible
champion of idea, lie, truth, platitudes, battered jargon,
giant & dwarf altongue—
Paragnosis, splacturion, Spirit of the Barns, E A G L M D S,
O silver alphabet in joy full return
to every tribe fresh and raw, clothed in animal,
scamping swamps and forests, bear-baiting,
firth-skimping, death-brothering,
to Gaels hording across the August bar;
the Damnonian dusky promontory haycocking,
setting hammer,
breast-rattling sun-shrieked beakers & horners, Cantii,
massed visage, Wotin, hark! The England stretches
away.

Bygone service, settlement mighty and sure,
Trinobantes herald toward Essex, Middlesex,
directionward;
Iceni to Norfolk, Suffolk;
Cassii to Herts, Bucks, Bedford, onward; Coritani beaconed;
Brigantes angled, and lo, the Belgae
set their tents for settlement's end—
The memories of all the years of that beginning,
the hunting, the hawking,
weaponed men and free-necked men;

legs clothed in red and blue, bandaged crossways from
      ankle to knee,
         the horned hat, the fierce braids and whiskers,
            fur smell, rawflesh shields;
chiefs dreaming heaven a vast hunt and feast,
         fearing hell an endless 4th season;
      and ladies in tight bodices fasten their mantles
            with wrought butterflies.

From **HERALD OF THE AUTOCHTHONIC SPIRIT**

Columbia U Poesy Reading—1975

What a 16 years it's been
Since last sat I here
with the Trillings again seated
he older . . . sweetly sadder;
she broader . . . unmotherly still

with all my poetfriends
ex-wife & forever daughter
with all my hair
and broken nose
and teeth no longer there
and good ol Kerouacky . . . poofed into fat air
Eterne Spirit of the Age . . . a
Monumental loss . . . another angel
chased from the American door

And what the gains?
Al volleyed amongst Hindu gods
then traded them all for Buddha's no-god
A Guggenheim he got; an NBA award;
an elect of the Academy of Arts & Sciences;
and the New York Times paid him 400 dollars
for a poem he wrote about being mugged for 60 dollars
O blessed fortune! for his life
there is no thief

16 years ago we were put down
for being filthy beatnik sex commie dope fiends
Now—16 years later Allen's the respect of his elders
the love of his peers
and the adulation of millions of youth . . .

Peter has himself a girl so that he and Allen,
Hermes willing, might have a baby
He's also a farm and a tractor
and fields and fields of soybeans
Bill's ever Bill
even though he stopped drugging and smoking cigarettes
Me, I'm still considered an unwashed beatnik sex commie
        dope fiend
True, I don't bathe every day (deodorants kill
the natural redolence of the human form divine)
and sex, yes, I've made three fleshed angels in life;
and I'm as much a Communist as I am a Capitalist
i.e., I'm incapable of being either of 'em;
as for Dopey-poo, it be a poet's perogative

Dear Audience,
we early heads of present style & consciousness
(with Kerouac in spirit)
are the Daddies of the Age
16 years ago, born of ourselves,
ours was a history with a future
And from our Petroniusian view of society
a subterranean poesy of the streets
enhanced by the divine butcher: humor,
did climb the towers of the Big Lie
and boot the ivory apple-cart of tyrannical values
into illusory oblivion
without spilling a drop of blood
. . . blessed be Revolutionaries of the Spirit!

POEM

Summoned by the Muse
I expected the worst
Outside Her Sanctum Sanctorum
I paced up and down a pylon
of alabaster poets
known and unknown by name
and lauded and neglect of fame

I felt weak and afeared
and swore to myself:
"This is it! It's good-bye poetry for me!"
And the eyes of Southey
humbled me
into a nothingness
I braced myself
with self-assurances
muttering: "Being a poet
limits one's full potential;
I can ride Pegasus anytime I feel;
though my output has been of late
seldom and chance,
it's the being makes the poem
not the poem the being;
and besides, I long ago announced myself poet
long before the poem—"
The great Parnassian doors opened
I beheld Her and exclaimed: "Ah, Miss God!"
She beckoned me sit upon a velvety gold cushion
I sat—and at Her swan-boned feet sat three:
Ganesha, Thoth, Hermes,
and over a pipe of Edgar Poe's skullen ash
they blew a firey diamond of Balbeckian hash
"O charming poet-stud whom I adore
my Nunzio Corso Gregore
I twirl churingas, I sing,
you inspire the inspirer
for behold I am the Muse
and music is my sacrament
—I ask you, would you ever deny me?"
"Never!" I swore . . .
From Ganesha's curled trunk to Thoth's ibis beak
to Hermes' Praxitelesean nose She flecked cocaine
from the Dawnman's mirrory brain—
"Would you favor me your ear?"
"Happily so O sweet sister of sestinas"
"It's Emily, Emily D . . .

I implore you regard her chemicry
she who tested a liquor never brewed;
and Percy Bysshe, your beloved Shelley
who of laudanum did partake
. . . but I fear I'll embarass you
this question I would put to you . . ."
"O soul of Shakespeare, ask me, ask me anything . . ."
I could hear the silent laughter
of Her three messenger-boys
"I have no desire to upset you—"
"Ask; I shall answer"
"What thinkest thou the poppy?"
My silence seemed the lapse of a decade
The eyes of She and the three
were like death chills waved upon me
When I finally spoke I spoke a voice
old so old and far from the child I used to be
"Dear carefree girl of Homer, Madonna of Rimbaud;
morphia is poet-old,
an herbal emetic of oraclry,
an hallucinatory ichor divined by thee
as traditioned unto the bards of the Lake,
theirs and mine to use at liberty
but I am not free to be at such liberty;
the law has put its maw
into the poet's medicine cabinet
. . . I tell you, O sweet melancholy of Chatterton,
the forces of morality
and depresséd gangs of youth,
this God-sick age
and fields farmed by gangster farmers
prevents the poet ferret his mind
halts him his probe of the pain of life
. . . for consider, around that lake
Coleridge and De Quincy were spared
the Eldorado Caddie connection men
and every other Puerto Rican mother's son
has his stash of laudanum
—for me there is no Xanadu"

"I ask you: Do you favor heroin more than you do me?"
The three each held a bloody needle
each needle a familiarity
"Was I with you when heroin was with you?"
A great reality overcame me
huge as death, indeed death—
The hash, an illusion, was in truth myrrh,
and the cocaine, illusion, was the white dust of Hermes'
        wings
Again Her awful tone:
            "Do you love drugs more than you love me?"
"Yeah!" I screamed
"You have butchered your spirit!" roared Ganesha
"Your pen is bloodied!" cawed the scribe Thoth
"You have failed to deliver the Message!" admonished
        Hermes
With tearful eyes I gazed into Her eyes and cried:
"I swear to you there is in me yet time
to run back through life and expiate
all that's been sadly done . . . sadly neglected . . ."

Seated on a cold park bench
I heard Her moan: "O Gregorio, Gregorio
you'll fail me, I know"

Walking away
a little old lady behind me
was singing: "True! True!"
"Not so!" rang the spirit, "Not so!"

Sunrise

I am rich
I've used my blood
like an extravagance

An archetype of oralcry
whose silence
            smells of cheap wine
A poetman
become an olding messenger boy
O silver tongue of spiritus!
I whoop it up
    in all my wealth
            like Great Mercurio
                twirling his white ribboned caduceus
                        in heavened air

Bathed & gowned
            by the Pigs of Prophecy
Asoak in a tub of soft flashes
        I step into talaria
And into my hand
            the twined winged wand was wound

I sat on the toilet of an old forgotten god
and divined a message theron
I bring it to you
    in cupped hands

...FALLS THE SUN LIKE A shot circle

Sunset

At the gate
  of the wood
    where the father
      nailed his antlers
        lies the snake Emeritus
          the Blue Stamp
            of the Virgin Wicce
              'pon its head

The alien son rubs against the tree
                lustily
And the She of Days
  holds a long Russian cigarette
            in her long hand
              humming a sura

Falls the sun
      s l o w l y
      like
      a
        shot circle

I Met This Guy Who Died

for J.L.K.

We caroused
    did the bars
        became fast friends
He wanted me to tell him
    what poetry was
        I told him

Happy tipsy one night
I took him home to see my newborn child
A great sorrow overcame him
"O Gregory" he moaned
        "you brought up something to die"

Earliest Memory

What's the first thing you remember?
How old were you?
And at what age did you realize it?
Or had you always remembered it?

When I was two years old
a wondrous thing happened:
Bereft of the woman from whom I was born
I was given to a woman
whom I believed to be my real mother
A one-year-old foundling
I lived with her for a whole year
During that year I distinctly recall
sitting in a bathtub with her
In the unforgettable silence of nakedness we sat
facing one another
My eyes steadied upon the hair between her legs
which was half submerged in water

Thus a double source of birth
recall I
primordial and contemporary
Water & womb
I beheld
that from which we're born
abathed in that from which all life came

What the Child Sees

The child sees
the foolishness of age
in a lazy wiseman—
the knowing depth of the child's eyes
innocently contemptuous of the sight

He knows foolish abandon
when it sits beside him
—senses the neglected wisdom
the spiritus not present
and suffers the proximity
of the nullified moment

Wisdom

I feel there is an inherent ignorance in me
deep in my being
to the very core
I know its presence
by an unforgettable smell
        first experienced in childhood:
A nose clogged with blood
        mixed with the odor of an old man's belongings

For Homer

There's rust on the old truths
—Ironclad clichés erode
New lies don't smell as nice
as new shoes
I've years of poems to type up
40 years of smoking to stop
I've no steady income
No home
And because my hands are autochthonic
I can never wash them enough
I feel dumb
I feel like an old mangy bull
crashing through the red rag
of an alcoholic day
Yet it's all so beautiful
isn't it?
How perfect the entire system of things
The human body
all in proportion to its form
Nothing useless
Truly as though a god had indeed warranted it so
And the sun for day the moon for night
And the grass the cow the milk
That we all in time die
You'd think there would be chaos
the futility of it all
But children are born
oft times spitting images of us
And the inequities
millions doled one
nilch for another
both in the same leaky lifeboat
I've no religion
and I'd as soon worship Hermes

And there is no tomorrow
there's only right here and now
you and whomever you're with
alive as always
and ever ignorant of that death you'll never know
And all's well that is done
A Hellene happiness pervades the peace
and the gift keeps on coming . . .
a work begun splendidly done
To see people aware & kind
at ease and contain'd of wonder
like the dreams of the blind
The heavens speak through our lips
All's caught what could not be found
All's brought what was left behind

For Miranda

My daughter
walks in grace
like a sharp New Yorker

I dream a dreamy child
in sandals of gold
walking the ramparts
of a Frankish tower

The Templar
kneeling by a streamlet
raises a handful of water
to his visor'd mouth
—there are white horses in Manhattan

The Leaky Lifeboat Boys

Waiting for the world
not themselves to die
they scheme upon getting out of life alive
"Dead we couldn't make it out of Hoboken yet"

They don't trust death
"It's a gimmick" they say
fobbed on them
by that most unreliable of species, humankind

Humans unanimously agree
in time we all must die—
They disagree,
To them death's the oldest gossip in planet town

Their Christian parents believed
their deaths would get them out
There was Heaven there was Purgatory
even Hell
any one of the three spelled OUT
"Sheer lunacy!" these sons harped
"If you wanna get somewhere you get there alive
dead you're up shit's creek!"

These men are educated
enough to know
it be the living not the dead
that go
to all those dreamed of places
bound & unbound
say: distant Proxima Centuri via rocket hurl
or instant earth via out-the-window

These darling men ever getting older
are insufferably ass-bound
claiming the planet like the body
is a leaky lifeboat
and with a tinge of urgency, cry:
"It's bail out time, we gotta mutate!"

The desire to mutate mutates
'tis the fuel of evolution this desire
You see, it's not that they want to live forever
they believe they are forever
it's just the form they're in and on
that's deathable

They view the prophets of lift-off with
understandable envy
"Just looka Elijah! Mohammed! the others!
        they made the out-of-here alive!"

Of the three leaky lifeboat boys
one is of a considerate nature
. . . wondering how the planet as well
        can get out alive

How Not to Die

Around people
if I feel I'm gonna die
I excuse myself
telling them "I gotta go!"
"Go where?" they wanna know
I don't answer
I just get outa there
away from them
because somehow
they sense something wrong
and never know what to do
it scares them such suddenness
How awful
to just sit there
and they asking:
"Are you okay?"
"Can we get you something?"
"Want to lie down?"
Ye gods! people!
who wants to die amongst people?!
Especially when they can't do shit
To the movies—to the movies
that's where I hurry to
when I feel I'm going to die
So far it's worked

Inter & Outer Rhyme

Last night was the nightest
The moon full-mooned a starless space
Sure as snow beneath snow is whitest
Shall the god surface the human face

Youthful Religious Experiences

When I was five
I saw God in the sky
I was crossing a bridge
on my way to buy salt
and when I looked up
I saw a huge man
with white hair and beard
sitting at a desk of cloud
that had two gigantic books on it
one was black
the other white
Saturday I asked the priest
in the confessional box what it all meant
and he said:
"The black book is for all the bad you do
the white book for all the good
If the black book
at the end of your life
weighs more than the white book
You'll go to hell and burn forever!"
For weeks afterwards I assured myself
that buying salt was nothing bad—

When I was six
I saw a dead cat
I put a cross on it
and said a little prayer
When I told the Sunday school teacher
what I had done
she pulled my ears
and ordered me to go immediately
back to the dead cat
and take the cross off it
I love cats I've always loved cats

"But don't cats go to heaven?" I cried
"Thou shalt not worship false idols!" she replied—
I went back to the dead cat
it was gone
the cross remained
Fittingly so . . . that day the earth had died

When I was seven
I sat in church one Sunday
next to a fat little boy
I'd never seen before
He had a small glass elephant
cupped in his chubby hand
And it was during the raising
of the Eucharist
when he showed it to me
That's when it happened
I remember how fast it happened
He fainted
They carried him away
the glass elephant still in his hand
The part that scared me most
was when the two men who had carried him out
came back and sat beside me
one on each side of me
Was I next? I wondered
I who had seen the glass elephant?
I never saw that boy again
And to this very day
I cannot totally comprehend
what it all meant . . . if it meant anything at all

Dear Villon

Villon, how brotherly our similarities . . .
Orphans, altar boys attending the priest's skirt;
                    purpling the coffins

Thieves: you having stolen the Devil's Fart
And I stealing what was mine
(not because like our brother Kerouac said:
everything is mine because I am poor)
Rather: Nothing is mine, a Prince of Poetry
made to roam the outskirts of society
taking, if I needed a coat, what was taken
                    from the lamb

Killers: You killed the priest who slit your lip;
thus far in that respect I am unlike you
                    O thankfully so!

What sooty life, eh what, oh Villon?
An after-rain has laundr'd your day
blued is the white of it
Yet when O when
                    shall unsoiled navies
                    sail by again?

I know the same I knew before
Now I would less knowledge than more
for I know knowledge to be
such information as fattens memory . . .
aye, wisdom is a lean thing
for regard that head on his deathbed
hemlocking: "All I know is I know nothing"
You at least claimed to know everything
                    but yourself
I claim to know all there is to know
because there ain't that much to know

181

Proximity

A star
is as far
as the eye
can see
and
as near
as my eye
is to me

Many Have Fallen

In 1958 I took to prophecy
the heaviest kind: Doomsday
It was announced in a frolicy poem called BOMB
and concluded like this:
Know that in the hearts of men to come
more bombs will be born
. . . yea, into our lives a bomb shall fall

Well, 20 years later
not one but 86 bombs, A-Bombs, have fallen
We bombed Utah, Nevada, New Mexico,
and all survived
. . . until two decades later
when the dead finally died

Nevermore Baltimore

O blessed dowser of lustration
drawn from waters where the discriminate ibis drink
raise the gold trinkets of Azteca
from the graves of the ladies of Castile
and bring it to Baltimore
to Sabbathai's music store
and there reclaim Apollo's plectrum
Pan's syrinx

Mrs. Poe, a singer,
died from a busted throat
And Mr. Poe
died from a drink
for every vote—
The fop of Harvard
great-grandson of Calvert
tumbled the tumbler
with a twist of the wrist
and called the unnamed by name
With sand in his shoes he vomited on Maryland
and unable to call playmates
to come out and play
he summoned, instead, the moon for the coming Monday

The tarot lady in her costume store
is witness, can testify, saw the fall
of Satan's poet
in the gutter of Baltimore

She scryed her crystal
saw me leave the music store
the strings and pipes of dead gods under my arms
With an amethyst finger
she beckoned me enter the door
and take seat upon a triangular cushion
spiked to the floor
She knew
I celebrated my 38th year on Easter Sunday
a rare occasion indeed—
I heard tell of Sin and Nut
of Parsifal
and of which direction the eight wands flowed
And was shown
the child Poe holding a midget doll
"And this is the top hat he wore"
said she, twirling it
"Same hat outa which he plucked
the Mayor of Baltimore like a rabbit"
She plunked it upon my head
so big it covered my eyes
"You can't have it!" she yelled
and flung it over her shoulder into the pitch
"You would-be!" screeched she
"At least he knew a wicca from a wicce!"

When a Boy . . .

When a boy
I monitored the stairs
altar'd the mass
flew the birds of New York City

And in summer camp
I kissed the moon
        in a barrel of rain

Getting to the Poem

I have lived by the grace of Jews and girls
I have nothing
and am not wanting

I write poems from the spirit
for the spirit
and have everything

A poet's fate is by choice
I have chosen
and am well pleased

A drunk dreamer in reality
is an awful contradiction
Loved ones fall away from me
and I am become wanting

Self-diagnosis:
A penniless living legend
needs get the monies
or write more poems
or both
If you have a choice
between two things
and cannot decide
—take both
'Tis not right for me to be wanting

I take out my pen
I pee white gold
And on the wall
I write thereon:
It was there
always there
minutely contained
in a splayed hand

Outside
        a fallen swallow
                marks the Tuesday
O my heart! finally
        at long last
                I am at peace
The half-century war
        I hacked at
                like an Afric Bushman
                        hacking bushmasters
                                        is over

I will live
        and never know my death

Ah . . . Well

People . . . nobody loves them
not even people
Want of love
. . . no one owes anyone anything
Whosoever pays dues hasn't
(I know of no collector)
They pay themselves
Those who demand respect
are seldom deserving
—not to show disrespect is enough—
People love only themselves
and not too well
Love for another
either in passion or compassion
stems from the heart's desperate need
The universe is alone
and people are alone in it
The Pope doesn't really love me
nor I he
Christ, his invisible love
I knew for a lover too
People bring on fear and pity
I fear human fragility
I pity coolies of humility
It's always a bad day for someone
Pain, Death
The Big Lie of Life
The apothecarian earth blooms the poppy
at best

Spirit

Spirit
is Life
It flows thru
the death of me
endlessly
like a river
unafraid
of becoming
the sea

I Gave Away . . .

I gave away the sky
along with all the stars planets moons
and as well the clouds and winds of weather
the formations of planes, the migration of birds . . .
"No way!" screamed the trees,
"Birds are ours when not in transit; you can't give it!"
So I gave away the trees
and the ground they inhabit
and all such things as grow & crawl upon it
"Hold on there!" tidaled the seas,
"Shores are ours, trees for ships for ship yards,
            ours! you can't give it!"
So I gave away the seas
and all things that swim them sail them . . .
"No way!" thundered the gods,
"All you gave is ours! We made it all, even the likes of you!"
And so I gave the gods away

Galactic Birth

The de-opiated body
steams on the basement floor
in the New York July

Its hand reaches for
delirium's magnum .44
and shoots its head off
over and over again
Bang! Pow! Born! Brains blown!
Ziing! Blotout! Bloodbloom! Trainsthrown!

The billion'd cells
of this miserable meat-hunk
wire the brain
like an electrified cat
Guatemala bounces from cortex to cerebrum
Guatemala! Guatemala!
The stink of suffocated green
"No Mayans!" he screams
"I don't wanna see no Mayans!"

Again he knows the same green
the snake-priest in the grass knew
Again the obsidian knife
hovers over the fuming heart

A snapshot
shows him lying on the old floor
of an observatory:
a writhe of multi-cells
alleles and chromosomes

The mud-skinned astronomer sees
the birth of a crab-like nebulae
circa 1080 A.D.
slowly develop in a polaroid sky

In Praise of Neanderthal Man

In a birth old and horrendous
I heard in a basement in a dream
the birth-scream of mothers
bounce off the walls of sooty coves and bins

and saw there white-gowned doctors
yanking goat-legg'd infants
from out torturous vulvas
incessantly wheel'd in and out
by white-masked orderlies
all besplatter'd with blood & goat hair

and the nurses beneath each hood
choked in the thick air
piling the amputated legs
of this increate indecency
neatly
like cords of wood

Upon awakening
I flashed upon a photograph
seen long ago
in an old magazine
depicting all the bones
of millions of years ago
—ape deer aurochs bear
pony mammoth mastodon man—
all dumped in a common pit in a cave

And there were other photos
of other finds
Afric gorges Cretean wells Carib grottos
all revealing a common meal
eons of human skulls
with holes

skillfully flint-drilled by human hands
the brains long since sucked dry
like so many eggs

And more finds came to mind
from the tundras of the Neanderthaler
to the Caroline peaks of the Alpine
It is not known whether Neanderthal Man
ate of his own
or mated with those much taller
and together evolved into
great Paleolithian muralists
Yet unlike their brain-sucking forebears
and the soon to come Alpine eater of bears
they bound their dead with beast gut
from feet to head
lest the ghost escape
(first record of magic date)
and buried them beneath the ground
upon which they slept and ate

Know this about that hoary brutish
bow-legg'd miserable toiler
who to this day is deemed a stupid thing
unfit for survival
you who claim his seed died with him
nor ever did associate (much less copulate)
with such heir as Cro-Mag, son of bear
—to you I say Neanderthal
himself knew to sing
inventor of the churinga
(first musical instrument)
able to make the air ring
I say to you you can separate
the yolk from the white of the egg
yet without the one
the other is none

—so again unto you I say O thou bigot anthropology
deem not Sir Neanderthal a stupid thing
all milk and no cream
in his time
       throughout the world
             he was philosoph supreme

Destiny

They deliver the edicts of God
without delay
And are exempt from apprehension
from detention
And with their God-given
Petasus, Caduceus, and Talaria
ferry like bolts of lightning
unhindered between the tribunals
of Space & Time

The Messenger-Spirit
in human flesh
is assigned a dependable,
self-reliant, versatile,
thoroughly poet existence
upon its sojourn in life

It does not knock
or ring the bell
or telephone
When the Messenger-Spirit
comes to your door
though locked
It'll enter like an electric midwife
and deliver the message

There is no tell
throughout the ages
that a Messenger-Spirit
ever stumbled into darkness

PETASUS

WINGED FEET
TALARIA

MAGIC
CADUCEUS

CAPT. POETRY & HIS MAGICAL LYRE
& PEGASUS

The Whole Mess . . . Almost

I ran up six flights of stairs
to my small furnished room
opened the window
and began throwing out
those things most important in life

First to go, Truth, squealing like a fink:
"Don't! I'll tell awful things about you!"
"Oh yeah? Well, I've nothing to hide . . . OUT!"
Then went God, glowering & whimpering in amazement:
"It's not my fault! I'm not the cause of it all!" "OUT!"
Then Love, cooing bribes: "You'll never know impotency!
All the girls on *Vogue* covers, all yours!"
I pushed her fat ass out and screamed:
"You always end up a bummer!"
I picked up Faith Hope Charity
all three clinging together:
"Without us you'll surely die!"
"With you I'm going nuts! Goodbye!"

Then Beauty . . . ah, Beauty—
As I led her to the window
I told her: "You I loved best in life
. . . but you're a killer; Beauty kills!"
Not really meaning to drop her
I immediately ran downstairs
getting there just in time to catch her
"You saved me!" she cried
I put her down and told her: "Move on."

Went back up those six flights
went to the money
there was no money to throw out.
The only thing left in the room was Death
hiding beneath the kitchen sink:
"I'm not real!" It cried
"I'm just a rumor spread by life . . .".
Laughing I threw it out, kitchen sink and all
and suddenly realized Humor
was all that was left—
All I could do with Humor was to say:
"Out the window with the window!"

When We All

for Spencer Smith who died

When we all wake up again
death will be undone
nor the stain of killed & killer men
remain in the wash of the sun

In winter we fell
tumbling
like two shot ducks
from the sky; a dream—

Your blue Aztec aeroplane
landed my infant son
and I
safely

I wept to hear your son
tell me
your Miami landing
had you die

I too am crashing
crashing
. . . Ah, Spring will
          bring a smooth landing

Alchemy

A bluebird
    alights upon a yellow chair
—Spring is here

Feelings on Getting Older

When I was young I knew
      but one Pope
      one President
      one Emperor of Japan
When I was young nobody ever grew old
      or died
The movie I saw when I was ten
      is an old movie now
      and all its stars
      are stars no more

It's happening . . . As I age
the celebrated unchanging faces of yesterday
      are changing drastically
Popes and Presidents come and go
      Rock stars too
So suddenly have matinee idols grown old
      And those starlets
      now grandmothering starlets
And as long as I live
      movie stars keep on dying

What to stem the tide?
Cease reading newspapers?
Cease myself?
Yes, when I was young
      the old always seemed old
      as though they were born that way
And the likes of Clark Gable Vivien Leigh
      seemed forever
Yes, now that I am older
      the old of my youth are dead
      and the young of my youth are old

Wasn't long ago
          in the company of peers
          poets and convicts
          I was the youngest for years
I entered prison the youngest and left the youngest
Of Ginsberg Kerouac Burroughs . . . the youngest
And I was young when I began to be the oldest
At Harvard a 23 year old amongst 20 year olds

Alive Kerouac was older than me
Now I'm a year older than he
and 15 years older than Christ
In the Catholic sense
          I am 15 years older than God
          and getting older

Women . . . the women of my youth!
To think that once I wanted to give undying
          love to the beauty & form
          of a lady of 40 in 1950
I beheld her recently she in her 70's
          in a long black dress
          her once magnificent ass
          all sunken flat!
How cruel the ephemera of fleshéd proportion
Poor Marilyn Monroe!
No Venus she
The mortal goddess
          is but a hairy bag of water
—and so are we all
And stone goddesses even with all their amputations
          maintain beauty in their ruin

Strange too:
When I was 20 my father was 40
And he looked & behaved like he did
            when I was 5 and he 25
And now that in 2 years I'll be 50
            a half century old!
            and he 70
it's me not him
            always getting & looking older
Yes, the old, if they live, remain old
but the young, the young never remain
. . . they're the stuff what becomes old

No, I don't know what it's like being old . . . yet
I've a wife in her early 20's
And I've a son just two and a half
In 20 years I'll be 70
She'll be in her early 40's
And he in his early 20's
And it'll be the year 2,000!
            and everybody will celebrate
            drink and love and have fun
            while me poor me
            will be even more toothless
            and bony-assed
            and inevitably stained with pee

And yet, yet shall planes crash
Popes, matinee idols, Presidents, yet shall they die
And somehow with all this oldingness
I see with vintage eyes, Life; Spiritus eterne!
With all the comings come
and all the goings gone

For Lisa, 2

I saw an angel today
without wings
with human smile
and nothing to say

A Guide For My Infant Son

Simple perfection
Perfect simplicity
It's easy
like painting a flower
or
snapping it dead

PREVIOUSLY UNPUBLISHED
POEMS

Rembrandt—Self Portrait

When I draw the magnificent Dutch girl
When I unshackle the peachwolf from browngold air
When I have the shepherd foxglove the chin of an angel
It'll make no difference whether I believe in God or not—

How do I paint the sorrow of men
—a group of singers lamenting the death of a friend?
Who stands so detached from life
and study if there be sadness in men?
Get me the saddest man!
Each brush stroke to break all systems
        the feeding circumference
    the spectric void—Devourer!
Paint! to compel hypocrisy
the face of the human
        become the face of the inhuman
get me gold linen! cold jewels!
        let me lightdrench the saddest of men—

Emily Dickinson—the Trouble with You Is—

Stop mounting pain
      If centuries—

The tight freeze of your flesh does not allow you transport
The cow is dead stiff—Do you stir
      You all alone by your sick fire?

In an uncertain dwell of love
You hid yourself
      A thin hand in a foxglove—

You discovered something not new but new to you
Dark deep disturbing the discovery
You explored a circle stupidly!
Calling the sky brown
      The earth a little town—

For you snow was no visitor
      Nor admired more than rain—

Good lady I love you
I can't look at a fly with my obvious betterness
      And ask Why

One Day . . .

One day while Peter-Panning the sky
I saw
a man dying over the Eastern Gulph,
and I said to this man:
—The light that makes us a fiend of eagles
       has made our poor wounds an interval of clouds,
       slow and creeping, calm and sad,
       in this skyful dungeon of things.—
And he replied:
—The sky is awful! The sky undarkens!
       Hermes, his wingéd foot, rests old in China!
       Rests uncontested while cloudbuds burst
       and windleaves fall!
       While my tired hands hold back
       the violent skirt of night!
       While my moss-covered feet crush
       the seaports of day!—
I left the dying man, and he must always die,
for Solitude refuses to lower a gentle hand
              upon his long sad face.

On Chessman's Crime:

Be *abnormal sex* a crime?
Then be it everybody's crime—
The raped is the rapist!
Every fuck is a rape, a crime!

Gas chamber for every being
     who ever fucked or never fucked!

It's all *abnormal!*
The virgin is sick!
The whore is sick!
The cocksucker the cuntlapper, sick!
The sodomist the normalist, sick!
The celibate the cocksman, sick!
Yes! every man & woman who ever fucked, sick!
The fucked and the fuckers
The unfucked and non-fuckers, SICK!
To the gas-chamber with all of them!
O ugly black pig-milk-bred us!
Look at children! Look at them vile things!
How did they ever get here?

Each child is a dirty proof of us! of rape!
     of fuck! each child a crime!

Rid the world of them!
Cut off your cocks!

Sew up your cunts!
     and be done with these walking products of crime—

A Bed's Lament

Once a long time ago
I held a royal couple
I was straight I was strong
And every day ladies joyed to clean me—

And now
And now I stand in a dank room
with shaky legs and sunken back
And upon me day and night
A bony junkie dreams and pees—

Direction Sign in London Zoo

←⫸

Giant Panda
Lions
Humming Birds
Ladies

St. Tropez, Early Morning

How all night long I waited
dreamless and waves of ending—
The boats in low waters
are leaning on their sides;
black clouds and no sun;
a sleek Polaris slips by;
men are conspiring against men;
Bridget Bardot lovelier than death;
I feel and miss my friends of old—
Towards heaven we're going
towards heaven I'm told.

Berlin Zoo

1

O the great slaughter of kangaroos
shipped frozen to West Berlin;
how was it each occasion of all my zoos
I feathered my words
saying I never ate meat
when I've eaten herds.

2

The Berlin Zoo
has two pay entrances.
One for the West
and one for the East.
But after the tickets are bought
they both join at the gate
and stream toward the monkeys.

Vermeer

See him stand beside a tiny gate
Around him lazy dogs congregate
In bright windows above his head
girls with porcelain jugs pour milk
while lonely men with heavy knives slice bread
and older wives in secret feel their silk.

3

How new
to know the sky
not only up
but down too

Death is but is not lasting.
To pass a dead bird,
the notice of it is,
yet walking on,
is gone
but for thought
and thought is all I know of death.

America before Europe:
50,000,000 buffalo
    900,000 Indians

America after Europe:
    100,000 buffalo
    900,000 Indians

Reflection

Instinctive seers who abandon this lovely age
sitting harkingly with dinosauric gapes
at what seems drabdross and no escape
are but anxious terminators of epochs
who wait it out like Europe
seeing man's end in their own dying.
Life a universal deathrow
such seers deem it so.

Commission Unfulfilled

Field Marshall Hawkes is finally happy
By order of the Queen
his portrait will hang in the Royal Academy

But midway the painter died
A portrait undone!
How often life wears itself out
expectedly   unexpectedly
but out   but the inconvenience of it!
The good-lord-what-a-time-to-croak of it!
Where the nose that smelled the foe?
Where the mouth that gave the command?

Apples

In this lovely lonely orchard
perhaps stemmed from Eve's core
I move in applelight continuum
of no dimension no dominion
And these apples whose certain death breeds more
has me reach for that out of reach one
and quite make it

30th Year Dream

I dreamed a man unknown to me in a city no
where on earth   I am the architect of that elsewhere world for sure
he was tall and a long black beard,   and he stood in a tall hairy
coat and Polish Rabbi hat he told me 'Christ wants to
see you' handing me a piece
of white paper with an address thereon   I refused it
happily (or was it smat-alecky) refused it telling him 'Like
I know where He/he lives,   And away I
skipped down a winding street I don't remember getting the asphalt
for and when could I have steam-rollered it?   still
I am the architect of elsewhere world
and the way the Lord built this here world
is the way I, in reams build . . . I think therfore it is
or I dream therefore I build (?) Anyway away I skipped into
an earthless yet familiar direction (where a place is familiar)
to me yet not of earth must mean that I possess recall of all
these people and streets and buildings created by my
dream's mind) but soon found myself looking for His
name on the directories of huge buildings all looking
alike deadend lost   O   how   I
trembled to see the look on my face when I ran back to the tall
man no more there   that look of a smart-alec struck dumb
with blix-eyed surprise   the agony of self-contempt
woke me up cursing me hitting me spitting on my legs 'Damn
impulsive goon-faced proletariat-Shelley greaseball dopey fuck!
And cried, 'denied . . . denied . . . denied'

There's a chineseman in my dreams

The Doubt of Truth

In the Muse
there is no rest home

And my vanity chest
is on the sidewalk
—the mirror broken

I look and see
a used-up poet
—what a sweet-sad
demolition is the poet-man

My good heart says: "No,
          silly, it's the mirror
                    what's broken"

Though truth is no longer my master
I will not entruth lies

I left my chest of poems
          forever
but returned the next day
and saw a Chinese man
          crying in the sun

The Doubt of Lie

Was humankind told me
I had to someday die

I don't trust humankind
They hurt one another
And are quite unreliable. . .
So how can I believe
that someday I'll die

The sun I don't even trust
—can blow up any time

And how can I trust them
who pollute the sky
        with heavens
the below with hells

Was humankind infested the woods
        with goat-footed drunks
Aye, humankind what unleashed
        its mythical zoo
against the sky
the monsters forever constellated

And meanwhile
     the last of the blue whale
is being butchered
          in a dying sea
How can I
throughout this cosmic scandal
          die?
Well, humankind,
     I'm part of you
and so my son

But neither of us
     will believe
     your big sad lie

Window

I say unto you
to die, to believe you die
is an awful, sad belief
People are unreliable
and your parents your priest your guru are people
and it is they who tell you that you must die
to believe them is to die
Because you see another die
you believe you must die
yet you'll only know the death of another
never your own
even in your cancer bed
you'll never know you wake up dead
The body is but a relay
we are born of ourselves
from incarnate dawn
to disincarnate night
to reincarnate dawn
an endless connection
the thread of which is spirit
Again I say unto you
I do not know impermanence
I am only with permanence
and I have contempt for death
I can only feel for the living
I cannot feel for the dead
They tell you that you gotta die to get to heaven
fuck those unreliable fuckers
with their fraudulent faith
killing eons of billions
I say to you dead: you ain't going nowhere
only alive will get you here, there, anywhere
The spirit knows better than the body

To believe that life dies with the body
is to be spirit-sick
This is the great danger
to body-think the spirit an ephemeral thing
The cancer victim of healthy spirit
is nothing terminal
whereby the body of health
dim of spirit, is—
As the fish is animalized water
so are we humanized spirit
fish come and go   humans also
the death of the fish
is not the death of the water
likewise the death of yr body
is not the death of life
So when I say I shall never know my death, I mean it
with me the spirit has surfaced the human face
I have gotten out of life alive
And don't let a dead body in a grave
marked Gregory Corso
make you laugh "har har,"
"and he said he'd never die,
looka the schmuck buried dead"
Just know that there'll be a sky
above that grave there
and it'll move the size of my spirit, everywhere
and this, only a supposition, for
you may never see such a grave
surely I'll never see it
So as the fish is unto water
so am I as well unto earth, fire, air
and not until all such elements
be no longer there
Shall I have indeed died
until then shall I yet be
like now, with the morrow
as I was with yesterday;

goodbye, have a good life,
remember that people are
quite often unreliable,
and it's them, tell you, you gotta die;
be seeing you on the rebound

Hi

There is no god
the likes of Mary, the blond hit girl
1st in her class at Vassar

There is no god the size of joan crawford's mouth
which in death smiles in dust
like a line of coke

There is no god
ever bewailed the dinosaur
more than the sincerest guy
in the creepiest bar in Baltimore

There is no god
like Mozambique Mort's god
except perhaps for Iwo Jima Jennifer's god
or Abyssinian Al's god
or Sumerian Sid's god
or
there is no god
the day after Milwaukee
No god
fifty years after the milk spilt
No god
greater than
the arrogant beauty queen of america
in a bmw car crash

Without god
the rev Jerry falwell
could very well be putting onions on the hamburgers
of the patrons of the White Swallow bar

Without god
the eons of billions of dead believers are fucked
With god
the billions of living believers suck

Why should there be a god
for the likes of you and me
when the caveman
never Billy graham's god knew
nor was a caveman ever a jew
Prove to me there is a god
stands between the wrinkled assholes
of a Rex Roberts and an Oral Humbard
I can prove there is no god
from Missouri
I come from New York City
—as if Jehovah witnesses cared

How can there be a god
when donkeys prefer straw over gold
and people knowing better prefer gold
and running with it get shot in the legs
When chickens eat hard boiled eggs   and
surely there can be no god
when Gregorys are called Gregs

Love Poem for Three
for Kaye & Me

—and whomever it may come to be

I'll dress you
in anything anytime anywhere
with damask spins of raiment
and fillets of vair

and undress you
your regnant adornments
passionately renting it to shreds
leaving you naked in blacken air
torc'd with golden Assisi's

then have you wear
for chastity's sake
clanky underwear

In daylight walk
a gentleman by your side
I'll be
yet come nightlight
a beastie in me you'll see
not the pigkind rolling in mud
. . . you'll know, my dear sweet wicce.
what kind
when your openings take
my thiefy wand of blood

Ah . . . then we'll pillow talk
the night away
'pon such things
as never left
or came to stay

O sweet sack
where our hearts
submerged
breathes

the continuum
by thy behest
I bequeathed—

Noted for Having Hard Heads
(Testa Dura)

la mia testa e una testa delicata

Halcyon stupidities
     flock my brain
where gone my former
     happiness
when wisdom
     solsticed my brain
so propitious for
     labor of words
O great fart of sky
I did see beforehand
     thy light

Clouds are envelopes   of water
     made of air
       casting fire
That's what I mean by
O great fart of sky
Shoe-shine boy of the gods
     am I
after all it was me
who sat on the toilet
  of an old forgotten god

With love, by the thought,
     the blue-drap'd mountains
and the descending cypresses
move unmoving
     for my loving eyes—

And the storms,
the battering clouds
like great horned sheep
proving their love
        to the girl clouds
—making babies
        of rain

Fire Report—No Alarm

And that I did not adhere
    to any man's God
neither a comprehensible
    Absolute
nor the inexplicable
    unseen breath
      of Omnipotent power
—that I did indeed feel
    the awesome lack
that in Heirophantic
    ardour
      is awesomely contained
and did not fall to
    my knees
    in abject piety
or even for a failing
    moment
give in
    to the warmth
    and secure
of God-embracement
—that I did not adhere
    to arcane trinities
or bow to lettered
    ambiguity
so that my soul
    be stenciled
    in wanton faith

—that I stood
　　　amongst the brethern
and aided the old
　　　and poor
as well the young
all for whom I
　　　did open the door
like an act of Jesus
Such be my metaphor
who with autochthonal
　　　spirit
stands before the
　　　universe alone
God-free
　　　father of my Children
and upon my finger
　　　the ring of poetry—

Poet Talking to Himself in the Mirror

Hi, I'm me—
It has become glaringly absurd
this hunt for me
believing that when I was
hunted down
I'd find not only me
but a whole herd
past me's, future me's
the whole cart load
and all the years
and where have I gotten to
in this point of time
this isn't the same mirror
    I gazed into years ago

      It's the mirror that changes
      not poor Gregory

Hey, in life
  Where I went, I went
  Where I stopped, I stopped
  When I spoke, I spoke
  When I listened, I listened
  What I ate, I ate
  What I loved, I loved

But what about
   where I went, I did not go
   where I stopped, I moved on
   when I spoke, I listened
   when I listened, I spoke
   when I fasted, I ate
   and when I loved . . .
      I did not want to hate

Now I see people
   as police see them

I also see nuns the same way
   I see hare-krishnas

Ain't got no agent
can't see poets having agents
Yet Ginsy, Ferl, have one
and make lots of money by them
and fame too
Maybe I should get an agent?
   Wow!
No way, Gregory, stay
     close to the poem!!!

Field Report

Night dies into dawn
like a great big yawn
I'm out in the field
making my report
Who/whom do I report to, you wanna know?
Aren't birds spies?
They report to the trees;
the trees report to the wind
and the wind reports to everybody—
But it's always the same message
That's why this report . . .
It breaks the monotony
I see the same birds see
We just deliver differently
Anyway I'm out in the field
and you should know it ain't easy
—o'erhead bullets whiz by
they're not real, them's poetry bullets
It's the Muse, who else?
out there on the firing range
She's got Pegasus with her
He warning everybody DUCK
I scream GO TAKE A FLYING FUCK
She laughs
I knew it'd make her laugh
No, it isn't easy at all
especially when I have to contend
with my particular worldview

O my god! there goes Kelly
you don't know him
I do and he's gonna die
he's no longer a Buddha belly
there's about ten gallons of water

MUSE ON FIRING RANGE

he's carrying like a pregnancy
There's Captain Bill
. . . shadow of me over the hill
In two weeks he'll be dead too
It's hard
to talk truly to God
to tell what you really feel
all with a straight face
Then again
when was it when
Sumer? We're not talkin' Sumer
Ah, for the purpose of rhyme
Kelly, it's a tumor
hath bloated him thus
And Capt. Bill, old age
simple, cut and dried, old age—

No, I wasn't born March 33rd
Yes, I am on the selves
up there amongst Fitz Roy's Beagle
and Arthurian elves
True, I boast an encyclopedian mind
and in the Encyclopedia
my name you'll find
I can go far
but never as far
as to accuse myself of hypocrisy
Look at Euripides
you think some smart ass D.A.
knows more than he sees?
And here
here in the sun-setting dawn
I see all the wonders
and weep for my life still in pawn
. . . scraps of paper
'pon which are scrawn
insensible ditties;
DaVincian smiles;
as well

glyphian geometries drawn
—for a shot
pawned 'em all;
don't tell me you're no hypocrite, Gregory
I'm no hypocrite

I stood in the Piazza Colonna
(my mother's maiden name)
on the Via del Corso
(my mother's wedded name)
Does that tell you something?
If not Gregory am me
why then all them beautiful kids
waving me?
A circle's empty
like long ago in the bud
Peace! May my bomb be a dud
Peace! O world hold thy mud
Peace! I was right having children
Who disturbs the peace?
Who be these beings human
our destiny at their unreliable fingertips?
Never did I imagine life smarter than me
When a child
I read in the Daily News
that the Lone Ranger had died in a carcrash
Imagine how perplexed
when the very next night
I heard him Hi Ho on the radio—
I wish I knew what time is waiting for
—waiting brings on the demons . . .
O mothers of families!
I'd never leave them in the lurch—
even if I'd have to start all over again . . .
Some think I'm after the answer
(you know, the when what who why bit)
No way, I'm no mouse chasing it's tail
I'm just a little orphan boy gone old
I've no mamma, no papa, no dente, no casa,

no bella donna, no dio, solo Io!
See now?
See how I play my woe?
A gratuitous fool I'm not
—at dawnbreak by the East River
I saw who it was
MOTHERFUCKER! the disturber of the peace, screams
The servants of society,
the darling boys in blue,
mace and billy club the crazed creep—
The populace gathers
who can breathe air
that emits from intensified gossip?
I can't bear tenement ladies gone fat
clucking in drab print dresses
all with the same dry grey hair
A poet who mocks the masses
is no better than that young blonde poet
with a snarl on his face—
such kind of behavior wouldn't do for the Muse
She wields a hefty A.K.

Shiver! Abandon!
damned furnished rooms!
Prisons! damn
pacing up and down, up and down
damn eternes of facing walls
hours on hours, and me
never having been on the moon
—away with me!
but I'm indispensable without me—
When you're an orphan you need you
That I've attained fatherhood
I am graduate of orphancy—
I put in my report: (just for fun)
There are no mysterious connections
no frivolous attitudes
no fashionable laxities
screw pre-arranged death days

242

ah, this tract this night
I in Rome in all my light—
yea this levity, brevity, frivolity,
so free and easy, cavalcade of good cheer!

I spew your beauty
I without brushing against anything
carefully do I tread carpets
you crasher of life!
Hey, but I love you, you know
Though you've killed me in my teens
I'm still that Nunzio
19 and raring to go!
Could well be my birthday falls March 33
O the untidiness of my room!
Where's my wife? Where's the broom?
Patronizing the Muse, it shows no class—
It's all my doing
Who do you think did this and that?
Who else zoomed my heart romantic?
No tailor donned me in velvet capote—
O lightweight
crossing Ponte Angelico
I figured the fine imagistic thought just thought
We shall survive the hurried memory of what we see
and yet
yet was it so
be there Gods?
the Gods know—

O death, I'm tired . . .
of fobbing you off 37 per cent of the day
What a lousy undertaker of the world I'd make—
The trouble was:
I was too real and death wasn't
I just thought
my trying to make head and tail of it—
was philanthropy

O soft dark, the past
master of stirring the nerves
cold and terrible
releases our grasped hearts
like clenched velvet—
This master, so opera-prone, solitary
ever with a smile for everyone
he's as mysterious as life chooses to allow
he's nothing but to marvel at
and when the kettle steams
and the woman shudders in the Irish bog
brain beware! witches abound
there's a warmth in the electrical impulses
danger thought! think ice cold blue
and the pump will automatically shut off
think thus! and the comatose thing will die
O merciful philosoph thou!
and when they come for the body
like a procession of Egyptian priests
the dynamos shall roar
and the bubbling wax foam
and the winds shall tap the glass
and swords resume their clash

I'm tired of this report
I'd rather be playing black jack
but I'm a devout sort
devoted to Mercurio
the greatest messenger of them all
in Greece they know him as Hermes
in India as Ganesha
in Egypt as Toth
in Israel as Moses
in Scandia as Loki
    in the Northern reaches as the Bellosurian arrow
in America as CBS

But the weather always comes in a moment
but again, that's another kind of report

which, thank Hermes, I'm not into
Should I question I wonder
whatever happened to the Lackawanna?
Many Koreans out there
clipping rotten grapes from bunches—
The blacks are sleeping
on cold old grey-dirty subway walkways—
Ah! here be the terra-cotta anus of a gold aphid—
that should enhance my report somewhat, eh what?
Take an Etruscan subway ride
in a terra-cotta car
let the newly-buried gold slide
into a grandma mason jar, har-har
the gold 6's
are horned 9's
—the oval dab
the offal of scarab—
What better than having an owl in the house?
oh, great, here comes the frucated heart man
having finished his rap—

Hmm, the neo-Etruscan has bought a house
in old Etruria
guess what happens?
Guys come up from Naples
with shovels and geiger-counters . . .
Looking for buried funeral gold
they dig holes all around his house
He complains because his house is sinking!

Once again my birthday falls on thee
O day of resurrection.
Eostre day, day of egg's jubilee!
Do I recall, O yes I do!
that Easter day when all was come what may
1968 from the year to the day
March 26 human be-in day
and again

1989 of now March 26
resurrection again day!
Easter's no fixed day, Easter's mutable!
ah, to be born
to be resuscitate
to know come the morn
what's on the plate
and what one ate—
That child there
on the other side of the firing range
there's something so lovely
in its all-aloneness
the space that surrounds a crazy child—
A sadness of primal recall
remembering wet trees
showering our young huddled bodies
—not all the Athenians
from coastal city to coastal city are dying
yet many are falling in slow motion
like rows of condemned soldiers
holding hands before a mass grave
one after the other
shot from behind
damn this new pestilence!
The swiftness of it
with no time for sudden realization
and they are all young
and they are the cream of the crop
'Tis an antique pest
afflicts the avant populace
North to South, East to West
a seemingly moralistic contagion
primed to become legion
they fall, all blessed gifted ones
one by one, all so smart, so young
Due: a realer, truer Godness
one of hope beyond futility
beyond pain, fear, ignorance
Indeed life indicates more than living—

5 decades of change have I aged
The depression of the 30's
the great war of the 40's
the culture of the 50's
the crack in the consciousness of the 60's
the betrayal of the 70's
the pestilence of the 80's
Why children?
There is no forever child
there is but constant childbirth—
I wish she'd stick to bow and arrow—
The weird fame of catastrophe
brools thru the cafes
where a woosh of coffee
a tapping spoon
indicate typhoon—

A small fry runs counter to himself
There's a code of ethics in a wild shoot-out
Heart hit . . . bleeding squares of clotted gold . . .
We often think how difficult it must be
until along comes the Greek
every ready with his warn:
Beware me wearing shorts!
Why do they do that?
Why do they do anything?
I'd love to shove a rose up your heart—

The olding revolutionary
sinks in a sunken chair
twirling finger curls of hair
he noondreams an age ago
when all was what it seemed
and everything lit up
like a Caravaggio—
Head bowed
a man ripped-off of his Lennon
—the footsteps of an old march
jouncing done all done

Those are grey-hairs haloing a head
that once burst the wildest hair
His walls are posted with old proclamations
BE-IN GRATEFUL-DEAD HAIR
all yellowing . . . yellowing

Gee, here my grandmother went to bed
on sheep fur
and here my grandfather went to bed with her
he on her or visa versa
and together made her
my mother
no, sorry, him
made him my father
So here I am 58 years later
looking up at their cave
all covered with bougainvillea
I've no camera but memory save

Music enhances this flick
of toothsome smiles
and redolent garlic—
Dearest England
it's me
your endearing Yankee
Remember when I drove you up your tapistried wall?
Insisting lion & unicorn
were ere Horsa cum Alysford shorn?

And has not poetry given birth
        decade after decade
                to generations
of the human spirit divine
        whereby and from a renaissance of singers
                laureled the specialty of its time
Proclaim so . . . centuries after the dawn
        the noon of consciousness came
                nascent like a dream of reality
and whereby/from sprung the children of flowers

in the summer of love—
ah, forest, wherein the stoat throats the rabbit
where the source of all dread
has the salver in the wellspring
exhibiting the Baptists head—
aye, the godmad nurse the god-sick
Out of the pit of the midwest came Mr. Jones
and San Francisco gave him the Temple of God
Out of the cage of anti-society came the Manson
and San Francisco set the Christwolf amongst the flowry lambs
Out of the South came the cruel Tom
and the gentle city became his preserve
The sins of the land are expiated here
this city of Francis
The great expiator is an imitator
and the zodiac loon
cut the throats of its dwellers with a spoon—
This city of Athenians and poetry
aids and Ferlinghetti
are all what's left of it
Renaissance O merciful Renaissance—

When it happens there's a sudden click in the head
like a synapse's been spliced
and I am become free
of religious ecstasy
Scream in the night!
Awful dark night of the soul! at noon!
clutch!
fingers!
signs!
philosophies!
transformations!
I wasn't contradicting myself
when I asked Why can't I
impersonate myself?
I should fear for beauty
twirling dacoits in some terrible dance—
An image, off in the distance,

tall, lean, and feline
it's Shakespeare stalking a lake of steam . . .
Before his terrible green eyes
life like a mirror shatters
into bits of death
each bit reflects a fulsome lifetime—
Had I never been born
would Shakespeare a reality be?
And when I cease this sojourn
what then were he to me?
Friends fade
and few new ones are made—

From out an apse
a wriggling crucifix in a dead hand lay
Perplexed monks
clothed in heavy brown
nod their smooth heads in turgid sway
prayerful the hellsent gloam go away
Ostara! Ostara!
they cried   Ostara!
No one heard
—the courtyard was a-whirl with racket
a clothesline of kettles
and other utensils
bang—clanged in the wind
a riot of shrieking chandalas!
Asingeeeeeeeeeeeeeeee Heldlinge!
not the afflinge; the schretinge . . .
The field's uncommonly silent
She's racked her assault shooter
and the mad child has jounced away
and who in all my Roman dreams
sat in the atrium
head against the trellises
upon a hawk-clawed-footed chair?
All signs are here:
the child one used to be
walking round and round

silently with bowed head,
like a Mandarin in a courtyard—

Report: It was always New Yorker cartoons
never New Yorker poems—
Early in the game I always believed
it was right for poets to be hard on poets—
Ah, looka there
my old cute demon friend has entered the field
it be the Weedy Lyke toting
a Vuitton tote bag
with a New Yorker
all greasy under his arm
He probably digs New Yorker poems
. . . well, he ain't the demon of taste for nothing

Shredded shadows! Flimsical palanquins!
I know why Silas took Barabas's place
in Paul's sojourn
. . . ah, these spotted fabrications of poetry
this harsh flotilla of knowledge, truth . . .
Manticores are on the prowl
—even were I to guarantee
recognizable images, aver
concessions to a higher finer ideal
while yet retaining a semblance of romantic tyranny
I'd need not bolster whatever. . . .

Poor St. Agatha!
cherubic twits
holding plates of her tits—
Thru scientific halls go
learn to know
time comes on time
clock and kalend
the accordances of the sun
Fate comes when time beckons
your time is up
a matter of seconds

Take me to where
fabled horses are corralled
place me anywhere
the center is everywhere
pal me with the flying kind
that I go a-galloping across the sanities of paved air
clippity clopping upon cobbled clouds
incessantly fluttering
above and below the streaming angel crowds
dodging monoplanes, climbing biplanes
Have me kiss their soft wet noses
have me feel their hot puffs
of redolent breath
that I be odiferous of them
awash in their sweet sweat . . .
take me to where old wizened
        centaurs roam
that I hear their brawn converse
and be given key to a fiercer philosophy
—in pat reality I am without home
Have me mount an old Chinese centaur
with wisp-whiskered face
Cathay skinned
like an ivory sage in a china store—
I mount him
and lope a bridge
toward the gates of Tao
I pray the gateman
would my entrance allow

That I a naked Tartar to it seem
gripping its silvery mane that it rear
telling it You are my animal spirit formed in dream
then bend to bite its leathery ear—
I see all or all but all
the armied mounts of Hannibal
go down each in slow ballet
each in studied fall
then rise in ghost cavalcade, away!

The jockeys of sleep
atop each dream mount
. . . the mares of night
scree across the screen
of dreamer eyes

I do take little walks from myself . . .
at the moment I see myself
coming down the street
And as always
I patiently wait on some corner
for me to rejoin me

One day I just might
up and walk away

* * *

DISPATCH DISPATCH DISPATCH DISPATCH DISPATCH
. . . the draught of a spokeless space. . . .
. . . a point perfectly arching toward itself. . . .
. . .the workings of the wheel
flows from the wheelwright
all in slow steady pace
what comes first in the circle
comes last in the circling

. . . in an avalanche of small dyings
one tumbles gigantically
like an old Greek god . . .
with vast mind contained of all great Ionia. . . .
. . . with eyes the rosy hue
of Western dawn and dusk . . .
. . . with hair entwined of black forests . . .
. . . 20,000 ft up in the sky
the cargo door blew out
taking nine seated passengers with it
seven fell into the sea
and the other two
got sucked in the engine
Once, another plane crash,
two still strapped in their seats
went flying thru a dining room
where three old ladies
were having welsh rarebit
. . . Swallows like blitzing stukas
are attacking the cat!
. . . a parsec a sec! Zoom! Jim Blaze ACE
Yo! Striker of Fear!
you nightmarish Spook of unspeakable Doings!
. . . all the veiled configurations, backlogged
. . . across the street is the cell
wherein Peter was crucified upside-down . . .
They're clamouring again for the death penalty in NYC
Blacks need only apply
It's the police . . . they don't like being killed

Misery never had anything to lose
Vengeance serves no remedy
O the self-tyranny of ignorance!
The unkindnesses towards oneself and others
Guilt! sickening fear! what yuk!
There are 50,000,000 homeless
cats and dogs in America

One dawn
a multitude of variable thought
rushed to light
The mandril predicts with tomorrow's tongue
Judah is come!
Mo-jo mo-jo
there's a new lion in the kingdom—
When nothing is not so good
everything is not so bad—
Where to go after having gone?
The rich young American snorts his coke
while all great China sails inexorably by—
Wallow the babe in Medusa's spill
have its heel strike Pegasusian sparks
. . . soar with the wings of poesia
. . . the last imaginary possibility
needs enlighten the dumb kind
. . . rise from the heavy drear
of this purely realistic world—
Obsidian . . . marble
and spondylous shells
This field, this spread, this
epipaleolithic farm
from the coastal quays to the lower
and middle Danube basin
to the Marcia plain
emerge in the Dniesta-Bug region—
He's been found guilty . . .
In a small space
he'll spend big time—
Such imbalance is unnatural

The natural space best suited man
is the length of ground he walks
from dawn to dusk—
And bring not your Alhambra Decree
back to me
Much ado that 1492
haunts the goyim as well the Jew—
Where does it come from
all this hate and turmoil
in what inner vault
dormant like a virus
ever ready to surface
and blow our cool from us?
Are we the churn of alien substances
churning a cheese gone amok
fuming our nostrils and mouths and eyes
reeking murder MURDER—
Anger seems ready made
it cooks a man when displayed—
Bump into him
give but slightest whim
he's apt to cut yr throat—
In the coal bin
stench of rat
he hates himself so—
Those two bums there
they don't lie like
Corinthian pillars by the Mediterranean—

The salamander,
the half-submerged rock
upon which it stood
and the swirl of stream around it
. . . when it darted away
I saw more than tiny wet imprints of its feet . . .
I have some fundamental fears when—
She moans "cancer" in the most
irritatingly screechy voice

. . . what to say to her
right here in the middle of nowhere

They're dying, they're all dying . . .

What I know to speak
is sure and true
caught in a life
not many knew
Watch out one morning
Don't believe the sidewalk
Earth will shudder
and wind
a great wind can come
and blow everything away

The day after the laser
is how the red dot
got into the black box—
STOP Her mind flows her hand
in sure rolls of ink
upon bright command
With no time to think
she already knows
the connecting link
STOP She who in consequence divides
madness dear STOP resolving old schemes in brighter career
STOP in dumb duress and avaricious claim STOP
for heaven's sake stop

You, you I saw
from way back ago
You slid above the earth
both feet in air
never touching ground
like in a dream you moved wherever where
and found there enthusiasm for terror
its truth so laid bare
you could never for all yr life err

O finest of the wise
who saw where the sunset rise
Look to you what looked to him
Providence may take
what cannot swim
I am double the age of him—

The blast of a blue piss
in an old pail
tells all of genesis
and the drive of the nail
And when I meet God
I'll make as much sense
. . . like I don't owe god nothin'
nor it me—
Let secretive Freemason's spill the beans
and cash the Bank of God's check by any means
I don't care
in Catholic eyes I'm better
than the Grand Canaria
And me never having been 33 degree ever
That my grandmother was a cave woman
deems me sorely applicable
a Knight of Malta be—Speak of lineage!
I'd wash with them aristocrats
the bony asses of the poor infirm . . .
remember, poet is up there with king, emperor, Pope . . .

Pray tell me anew
that which I would
tell unto you
Doth the lowering
of voices and radios
excuse our peccadilloes
STOP O indomitable damp dogs!
Woeful unshaveness! defiant bellows! tresses
brooling in the fore rain

'Tis the woman in thee O brawny hood
inspires fascination for fear
a woman's fear is not as fearsome as man's . . .
There's no harder reality than realist woman
Nature insists thus
Were woman as haphazard as man
beware re-generation—
Man can fuck up, woman can't . . .
It's a losing game, generalization
yet I love being smart
when generalizing—
Terrible it is for a child-man
to give his loved one a child
. . . soon as she gets the kid
she drops the father, saying: Hey, one kid's enough!
Doesn't my grey hair
prove I'm grown up?
Someday I'm gonna fool everybody
and come on like Clark Gable . . .
He had false teeth, remember
the fanzines? when Hedda Hopper
said Vivien Leigh said
"His choppers smelled like a wombat!"
I predict Jeanne Dixon will die—
O would there a god I might love
One to offer prayers of marvel to
One in whom I may endow all such wonders
as greatworks of love allow
Were such a god mute
and I blind
I'd embrace the very air
and breathe the breath of its beauty
ah, this god so sod
O yea would there were a god
all new to me
untainted by Days of Old
bereft of human legacy
—Bright born
. . . sprung from womb of earth

the very pit of it
all a-dazzle in skin of air

If there were no calendar
I could have lived a million years
before my second year—
Born at the dawn
of remembrance
—what event unforgettable
occurred memorable?
The Sphinx came before me
yet were I never
no thing would come after me
Socrates, Christ-like
Shelley wrote great poems before Rimbaud at 16
The girls were never
seafaring men, brawny
leather-tanned, tattooed
Nay, they were mouse-eeked
dressed in teen-age Joan Crawford raiment
. . . with a hard mask beneath each orthodox face—
Girls, such humankind as can erect homo-erectus
by the mere wiggle of an ass!
What dire magic this?
Scholars, Greeks, painters,
people are downright embarrassing!
You wouldn't think the judge would, would you?
I mean not with him up there dressed in black
and you below guilty of god-knows-what
and he with IN GOD WE TRUST above his head—

The homeless are not beloved of god
Someday we'll all be homeless
I predict the mayor will find himself out on the street!
Ah, the far distant future . . .
I see a box sealed with a Knights of Pythias signet
within: pieces of tallow and vair—
Unoccupied rooms I see
And ugh to see one occupied

with fat sloppy him in it
all beer-cluttered
ughly him, lying in wait
for the strong strapping young
girls from the country

Future rooms! the size of 'em!
You open the door
and walk out the window
The homeless are occupying the benches
now the old have nowhere to sit—
That homeless one there
she's going to the toilet in front of everybody!
in broad daylight!
and that other one,
lighting up crack
. . . the dark is not done in the dark anymore
Why should they give a damn who sees
Once you show your homelessness to people
what's there to hide?
—a home, you can hide things—
Here be no fluted plain
here be a haggle of rapists!
And when had I last
moved into a new space
and covered the walls
with all my Wildes, Baudelaires,
Hugos—
There was a colder field . . . there where
frosted ladies
hung in Gein's shed like deer

Money does not come with instructions
When I get it
I get it with batteries included
Speak of burning a hole in one's pocket!
It just doesn't like hanging around me
. . . soon as I get it, gone!
Whoa, Ben, hold on a sec!

In a flash it ends up either
in some desperate black hand or
lobster for four—
I am truly ignorant money-wise
That's why I'm denied grants, etc.,
"a bottomless pit, that one,"
as if I don't travel, pay rent, eat, honor birthdays . . .
Sloppy.   Wow how sloppy I am with money!
Money in every pocket, no wallet, no clip
I just bunch it up and stuff it—
The back pocket, beware the back pocket
It's not a good place, I've finally learned
Each time I reach into it to pay
out falls, unseen by me, tens, fives, twentys . . .
once I turned around, and there was a fifty . . .
And O how physically peculiar money is!
I mean what it does to one's appetite
There I was, famished, broke
hadn't eaten in three days!
for two bucks I could have gotten
thick potato soup and buttered black bread!
But no, just my luck—I come into
600 dollars, and gone my appetite—
Whatever, it's not the moneys made
it's what's made what money buys—
for instance, so far I've earned 30,000
from 1958 to 1988
for my MARRIAGE poem
and to think I wanted to call it
EPITHALAMIUM—
It's not difficult at all to spot
a money-winner
They really look blessedly cool
Women know the value of a bought man
A bought man is married, evaluated by divorce
Or, she be childbearer peer; he
provider, blest of her and their child
No money truly has nothing to do with love

Many images tonight
—cocky me says they're all *la même chose*
I haven't been uptown yet
it's been years
2 years in Rome
and 8 months downtown
in good old Greenwich Village
What's uptown?
acquaintances
Classy . . . warm to me,
but acquaintances can never make friends—
Tell me
tell me why all the changes
change drastically
yesterday
yesterday everything was in place
including all the fuck-ups
. . . but cometh, Mr. Whirls

Fill the tub up . . .
to the knees,
measure water by the cup
whilst bathe-madens
escort Archimedes . . .
It's with how wide a third eye be
tells what you may or mayn't see
The finest arcana is seldom told
the Magus is a dazzling boy when old
Tap an Arab on the shoulder
and a Brazilian might turn and smile—
The body of man is with head of crocodile
Reflect:
the whole life of you is a battlefield
invisibilities armed to the teeth
more than Caesar's armies
engage. . . .
The wounded hand of war
holds an old black-silver wreath . . .

Arab & Israeli
both despair of pork
. . . so easy. . . .
Which one
as he walks away
would turn the sun
into another day?
The Semitic one . . .
Abraham left Ur
Ur was of Sumer
Sumer was non-semitic
ergo Abe were no semite
. . . look it up.
I would to Jerusalem have gone
a guest of the ancients
imagining Jeremiah everywhere
with tinhorn to ear
patrolling the genetic field of Genesis

Wind a spool of stellar string
into a round harmony
and throw it over a tree—
Have Lucretius look up
and wonder atomy . . .
Project two old men
in a desert, seated
—drier than the twisted steel
of an old train wreck
Hard it is for the heart to go out
to this heap of smashed men
pyloned along the subway way
like pieces of red-rusted junk—
What can save these men
Their faces are too far gone
they need more than a bath a meal a bed
These old broken ugly faces
cannot illicit pity even
there's no tragedy about them

they're finished, kaput, don't bother to look
Man is kinder than life
Man has heart, not life—
No wonder,
Life sees man come and go . . . endlessly;
for whom in particular should it care?
—two rats are nibbling pizza near the 3rd rail
I swear that wreck of humanity wished he had it instead
O rare beauty . . . I tell you smashed men can't weep
A time remembered, O mercy
. . . afternoons; a child's mahogany nap

Old age . . . it comes
like a stranger cat in the night
purring its head against your head
quiet old age . . . creeps up to you
like a bag lady
"Got something for me?"
I've yet to be smart about old age—

Something has lost itself
it was in me perhaps part of me
now it's gone
gone and I don't know where
don't even remember what it was
all I know is I suffer the lack
It's like if I died and returned
not to see anything familiar . . .
sometimes I get an inkling
it goes quick, and pleasant
like a childhood memory—
My youthful ignorance had all as FOREVER
Yes, true, we're going
it's always time to leave
. . . and if you miss departure
be sure there'll be another
Some I've seen anxious
muttering: Waiting brings on the demons!

yeah, sure, we're going
you didn't believe you'd remain here, did you?
"Well, immorality is young,
look at Mapplethorpe,
and young, face it, is ephermeral"—

It was Truman who said, "A man who doesn't dream
is a man who don't sweat"—

So fine a thing in life, dream
Three powers we got: Here and now;
what's imagined, and what's dreamed—
At least, that's the extent of my power . . .
I meant I dreamed the Acropoli before I made it to Greece
I was on the moon long before Neil Armstrong
That's the old playground of poets, the moon . . .

The reason why
is quite ramified
like when I die
you'll say I died—

Of what import is it I set things aright?
Who knoweth *niente*?
You bring Capital Punishment to this city
you'll have me poet of a dumb city—
That just don't sound right—

My son in my dreams is me
the dark nurseless room
the quick shadow
the small innocent head safe under the blanket
I am a father far away from his children
but like Holderlin sayeth I am closer to god
away from Him . . .

STOP

1989–90

DRAWINGS AND POEMS
FROM A NOTEBOOK
BY GREGORY CORSO

EARLY BEAT: During a break in the filming of the 1959 historic beat film, "Pull My Daisy," featuring an original music score by David Amram, who also appeared in the film, the composer (top right, hand to mouth) shares ideas with some of his collaborators, including (left to right): poet Gregory Corso (back to camera), artist Larry Rivers, author Jack Kerouac, David Amram and poet Allen Ginsberg. "Pull My Daisy" features Jack Kerouac's narration and a title song by David Amram, with lyrics by Jack Kerouac, Neal Cassady and Allen Ginsberg. (Photo: John Cohen)

Crowded round the table
Scholars, students,
Travellers
Poetic genoir Cetiques —
Ashtrays, Soy Sauce
Coca Cola
Pasta, Hummus,
Nitrous oxide —

Lots of gas, lots of beans
teeth & heads —
Have some beer
young Jonahan!

Think I hold
  the moon
as I would
Holy Communion
    on a
  basket ball!?
Dummies"!
It'd be the moon
  It'd be holding!
and for basket
it'd be my
    sky —
  Love,
    Gregory

Grumpy Buddha

allen's drawing

allen
as hard
on nails —

Gregory
Corso

Waking day before Xmas
old mss. to be reprinted
en masse —
old Kerouac Visions
Burroughs' epistles
Near half century antique
a flood of letters
old Bunny emotions
Nausea from Tangier
Truck tire ecstasies
of Wasatch Highways
Gay longings on top of Teton
Mountain skilifts —

Lets go visit Orlovsky in the
Madhouse today!

12/24/92 AG.

Will he wander in front
    of a dead truck?
Will he take a broken foot
    to kick in Richard's door?
Will he ~~xxx~~ write an epic
    about Hafcadio in Mexico?
Rescue Julien from silent cultural
    halls in Binghamton?
Go entertain a godling ghost
    in Louisville?
Settle down and marry an
    earthworm lady?
Never cantile in advance
what St Peter will do
    on Heavenly Geeches,

12/24/92 AG.

The Lamb lieth with the Lion

Gregory Corso

Dear ~~at~~ Roger — if I take my first
trip to the East — especially India
— me no longer ~~will~~ healthy
Gregory — 62 ½ years — my
Coy power may have dwindled —
Peter's not in best travelung
partner state —
Plus drugs — there be such as
I coocoon myself with —
no good for Gregory —
I got better I dea — why can't
Peter & I live together —
Say a thou a month place
— enough room — I'll
follow his Buddhist ways
if he allows me privacy to

NINA & GREGORY